AGAINST
PROFESSIONAL
SECRETS

AGAINST PROFESSIONAL SECRETS
(Book of Thoughts)

César Vallejo

Translated by Joseph Mulligan

ROOF BOOKS
NEW YORK

ISBN: 978-1-931824-42-2
Library of Congress Catalog Card Number: 2011920512

Translation editorial support by Abigail Méndez
Cover art "The Making of a Fresco, Showing the Building of a City"
    by Diego Rivera
Author photo by Juan Domingo Córdoba, 1929.
Book design by Deborah Thomas

ACKNOWLEDGEMENTS
I wish to express my gratitude to Abigail Méndez for her editorial insight, patience
and willingness to explore so many dimensions of Vallejo's writing. Thanks are
likewise due to Patricia Rossi who collaborated in setting the Spanish version and
weighed in on numerous unforgiving translation problems. I am also in debt to
Pierre Joris for helping me realize my role as poet-translator and for supporting this
project for the start. Finally, I thank my wife, Beatriz Sosa, who joined me in my
search for Vallejo's house and knocked with me until there was an answer.   *JWM*

State of the Arts This book was made possible, in part, with public funds from the New
York State Council on the Arts, a state agency.
NYSCA

Roof Books are distributed by
Small Press Distribution
1341 Seventh Street
Berkeley, CA. 94710-1403
Phone orders: 800-869-7553
www.spdbooks.org

Roof Books are published by
Segue Foundation
300 Bowery
New York, NY 10012
seguefoundation.com

Contents

Introduction

When we hear about César Vallejo, the image of the poet *por exelencia* emerges before our eyes. One of the giants. Not just the poet's poet, but the people's poet, too. Yet, few are aware of the breadth of the Peruvian's achievements as a writer and the scope of the man. Rarely do we think of his 244 articles, his 12 plays, his 7 volumes of fiction, 3 volumes of translation or even his 2 books of thoughts. *Against Professional Secrets* is one such 'book of thoughts', and it illuminates Vallejo's ideas and the trajectory of his literary production more clearly than any other of his works.

In 1923, Vallejo expatriated from Peru after publishing three major works of literature: *The Black Heralds* (1918), *Trilce* (1922) and *Scales* (1923). The latter two prefigure his project in *Against Professional Secrets* with regards to both form and content. The form that crosscuts these works is the prose poem—first used in *Trilce*, developed in *Scales*, and mastered in *Against Professional Secrets*. Thematically, the revolutionary spirit of the present volume can be traced directly to *Trilce* through the poetic treatment of human oppression.

In *Trilce*, the indigenous are represented as a symbol of marginalization. There we read about those "farmhands of sapient kin", those "blighting ploughtails [that] in spasm slacken". In *Against Professional Secrets* this symbol expands beyond the indigenous, encompassing the international proletariat. The symbolism of human oppression here acquires a more universal and socialist meaning. Those "fraudulent silence-due crusades" of *Trilce* have now transformed into "the regime of capitalist competition".

The remarkable collection, *Scales*, contains a section of prose poems called *Cuneiforms* that anticipates the thematic and formal thrust of *Against Professional Secrets*. In "Northwestern Wall" our narrator is imprisoned when his cell mate suddenly kills a spider. In this decisive event, Vallejo finds profound ethical meaning that leads him to conclude that justice is only infallible when it is not seen "through the tinted enticements of the judges". Vallejo levels the playing field by locating the problem with Justice not in its own nature but in its social application. Therefore, "no one is ever a criminal. Or we all are always criminals."

Against Professional Secrets furthers this concept of Justice in the prose poem "Individual and Society", where a murderer roams free for more than a week without hiding from the police. The authorities cannot find him because he is not hiding. "To this extent the individual is free and independent of society." Yet, one of the judges of the Tribunal gives off "an astonishing likeness of the defendant". The presence of his double guarantees his death sentence: "To this extent the individual conscience is social and collective."

While *Trilce* has come to be known as Vallejo's poetic adventure, *Against Professional Secrets* can be considered his meditations. The original manuscript bears the subtitle "libro de pensamientos" (book of thoughts), and rightly so, since it affords him an informal space to explore, interpret and analyze the meanings of a wide range of phenomena. The shift in creative process seems to be closely linked to his move to Europe. Fed up with the "provincial environment" of northern Peru, as he called it in a letter to Gastón Roger, where he served a 118-day sentence for a crime he did not commit, the poet left his homeland, never to return. Vallejo's arrival in Paris marks a turning point in his trajectory, and he enters the world of journalism in 1925.

The bulk of *Against Professional Secrets* was composed in 1923-1924, while he was getting set up in Paris, and then in 1928-1929, during his outright conversion to Marxism. The impact of traveling around post-WWI Europe, including three trips to the Soviet Union, cannot be overemphasized. In his book, *Reflections at the Foot of the Kremlin*, Vallejo writes: "On the day when the misery of the unemployed has worsened and spread, when the governments and employers have been exposed for their definitive impotence to remediate the problem... the masses clawing at the pastries of the rich will then be terrible, apocalyptic." The magnitude of Vallejo's journalistic output is astounding, as is the fact that so much of it is comprised of personal interviews with people from all walks of life. If we read those articles, it soon becomes clear that many were longer, more expository versions of the crystallized pieces found in his literary work.

The phrase "Contra el secreto profesional" first appeared as the title of a poetry review of *Ausencias* by Pablo Abril de Vivero in the popular magazine *Variedades*. Vallejo barely reviews Abril de Vivero's poetry, except for his remark that it possesses "a refreshing glow without pretensions" and "does not intend to discover the cure for tuberculosis or even another school of poetry". He devotes most of the article to an attack on avant-garde literature, enumerating several formulas that Latin

American poets were appropriating from the European tradition: "I raise my voice and accuse my generation of being unable to create or exercise a spirit of its own, made of truth, of life, of healthy and authentic human inspiration." Instead, he demands a new attitude, a "new sensibility" as he calls it here and in several other works. The following passage summarizes the strategy that Vallejo uses in what became the manuscript *Against Professional Secrets*:

> There is human tone, a vital and sincere heartbeat, which the artist should foster, though it doesn't matter in which creative disciplines, theories or processes... In the current generation of America, no one manages to have that emotion. And I single out those writers of gross plagiarism, because I think that their plagiarism stops them from expressing and realizing themselves humanly and highly. I single them out for their lack of spiritual honesty, because while they imitate foreign aesthetics, they're aware of their plagiarism and, nonetheless, they practice it, boasting, with insolent rhetoric that they create out of autochthonous inspiration, out of the free and sincere drive of life [...] Autochthony does not consist in saying that one is autochthonous, but precisely in being so, even when not saying so.

While the review of Abril de Vivero did not make its way into the manuscript, the title and Vallejo's position in it did. It is through this lens of autochthony that Vallejo's work must be read. Abril de Vivero was not the inspiration of this volume, but the living proof that modern poetry was still possible outside the sphere of the avant-garde. Auroral, not self-indulgent, Vallejo's poetry embodies a very different sensibility—one that can be brought into focus through a close reading of the title.

In the Spanish, "el secreto profesional" refers to the confidentiality between doctor and patient or attorney and client. In this sense, as a position against this oath of confidentiality, the title of the work could be translated as *Breach of Confidentiality*. Yet, "un secreto profesional" is also "un secreto de la profesión"; that is, a trade secret kept by the master technicians, the initiated members of an exclusive professional order. In this context, the title becomes an allusion to *Le Secret Profesionnel* (1922) by French Surrealist Jean Cocteau, who lays out his concept of the poet-as-angel and establishes a set of prerequisites that one must meet in order to enter the circle of the initiated.

Cocteau describes an aesthete who is loyal to the secret of his profession. His angel, a conventional specialist, sanctifies his poetic office,

isolated from and opposed to the rest of society. *Against Professional Secrets* attacks professional interest, trade secrets, professional confidentiality, and the notion of the sacred office so central to Cocteau. For Vallejo, the artist plays an integral role in the world—in concert with other citizens: "Sports should not be the art of the few, but tacit and universal attitude of the many."

The closer we read this book, the more apparent it becomes that Vallejo modulates styles to demonstrate this new sensibility. He adopts Romantic, Symbolist, Surrealist, Socialist, Realist, Scientific, and even Existentialist genres, as if to say '*how* one writes poetry is not as important as *what* one writes'. And he proves it by adapting diverse forms for his own content. What makes this argument so compelling is that, by modulating styles, he implicates himself in his own critique, widens the scope of his project and shapes a collaborative politics instead of the usual oppositional polemics.

This chameleonic strategy is evident throughout the book. In the virtually confessional prose poem, "Languidly His Liqueur", the poet does not search for a Romantic union with the Virgin, but rather turns his attention to concrete existence: "'Someone's knocking on the door!' my mother. / 'Someone's knocking on the door!' my own mother. 'Someone's knocking on the door!' my whole mother said." And she is "plucking her entrails on infinite frets..." as if they were a guitar. The music of his poetry comes from the bowels of humanity.

Now, contrast that mode with the Kafkaesque "Reputation Theory" where the police have just arrested a man for assaulting a public official, and the criminal's name remains unknown. What is this man's name? Neither he nor anyone else knows. There are no official records of him. Legally, this man does not exist: "The life of a man... is completely revealed in only one of his acts. The name of a man is revealed in only one of his signatures. To know that representative act is to know his true life. To know that representative signature is to know his true name."

Prefiguring the narrative innovations of the Latin American Boom, "Masterful Demonstration of Public Health" is a quest to describe a distant and fleeting memory. Yet, after repeated attempts the narrator recognizes that languages are part of a larger community. He abjures the concept of the "thing-in-itself" in order to examine relationships. To understand the event requires a multidisciplinary approach, namely, the creation of a vocabulary made of words from Russian, German, Polish, English, French, Italian and Romanian. Things don't stand by themselves. Therefore, only this "fickle polyglot lingo" can afford an accurate

expression of his memory.

Against Professional Secrets takes us on an aesthetic journey through 19th and early 20th century Europe, only to reveal that the poetic vehicles that have transported us are as arbitrary as they are exploitative. These meditations are at once an attack on the European avant-garde and an appeal to Latin American writers to quit the practice of aesthetic importation. By moving art from the realm of aesthetics to that of ethics, passing through the political economy, Vallejo lays the foundation for a poetics of human solidarity.

The original manuscript, *Contra el secreto profesional (libro de pensamientos)*, is stored at the Biblioteca Nacional del Perú in Lima. First published by the author's wife, Georgette de Vallejo (Mosca Azul, 1973), it has also been transcribed and published by Ricardo González Vigil (Editora Perú, 1992) and by Manuel Miguel de Priego (PUCP, 2002). I have consulted these editions to establish the Spanish version and have reconciled discrepancies between them. This book was never published in Vallejo's lifetime, and the manuscript itself was never completed. The original manuscript is more a finding than a polished totality—again, we are reminded that this is a book of thoughts. All of the manuscript contents are stored in box, and the natures of these documents are quite distinct. For the sake of clarity, the contents can be divided into three parts.

1) The first section is made up of the longer, more polished texts, most of which were typed by Vallejo himself and, in some cases, were edited by hand. 2) The second section consists of short notebook entries and loose papers thematically similar to the first part. Many of the writings in the second section were incorporated *verbatim* into other published literary works, thus confirming the idea that the book of thoughts was Vallejo's drawing board. Since he wrote *Against Professional Secrets* and *Art and Revolution* simultaneously, many of the short notebook entries were swapped between the two volumes during editing, but he never finished his deliberations. The sections of the notebooks that he wished to include in *Against Professional Secrets* are preceded by three pluses "+++". Those that could be included in either the present volume or in *Art and Revolution* begin with three question marks "???". 3) The third section contains "Notes on *Against Professional Secrets*" that according to Georgette de Vallejo, not always an accurate reporter, should be appended to the collection. These "notes", simply titled with roman numerals, are apparently topics for future research.

There are many ways to read Vallejo and any translation of this work in particular must address the deceptive simplicity of his writing.

As distinguished from *Trilce* and *Scales*, both works that flaunt their technical complexity, much of *Against Professional Secrets* is elegant, cautiously punctuated, prose poetry. It is paradoxically bold and subtle. It possesses a seeming transparency, a kind of gleam or finish, but we must not be fooled. Beneath that shiny surface, elaborate and complex turns of language await the tenacious reader, and these are as poetic as any line in his four volumes of verse. To glide over this poetically charged language is to ignore the semantic and phonetic generosity of the source text and the possibility of the poetry in translation.

Joseph Mulligan
New Paltz, New York
2010

CONTRA EL SECRETO PROFESIONAL
(Libro de pensamientos)

❁

AGAINST PROFESSIONAL SECRETS
(Book of Thoughts)

LA MAYORÍA DE LAS GENTES...

La mayoría de las gentes gusta ver el deporte, pero no practicarlo. Existen millones de espectadores en los estadios y apenas unos cuantos jugadores. La mayoría ama el deporte cerebralmente, cuando no literariamente.

Un día desaparecerá el campeón, para dar lugar al hombre en estado deportivo. El deporte no debe ser el arte de unos cuantos, sino una actitud tácita y universal de todos.

MOST PEOPLE...

Most people like to watch sports, but not to participate in them. There are millions of spectators in the stadiums, but only a few players. Most people love sports cerebrally, if not in a literary way.

One day the champion will disappear and give rise to Man in his athletic state. Sports should not be the art of the few, but tacit and universal attitude of the many.

EL MONUMENTO A BAUDELAIRE...

El monumento a Baudelaire es una de las piedras sepulcrales más hermosas de París, una auténtica piedra de catedral. El escultor tomó un bloqueo lapídeo, lo abrió en dos extremidades y modeló un compás. Tal es la osamenta del monumento. Un compás. Un avión, una de cuyas extremidades se arrastra por el suelo, a causa de su mucho tamaño, como en el albatros simbólico. La otra mitad se alza perpendicularmente a la anterior y presenta en su parte superior, un gran murciélago de alas extendidas. Sobre este bicho, vivo y flotante, hay una gárgola, cuyo mentón saliente, vigilante y agresivo, reposa y no reposa entre las manos.

Otro escultor habría cincelado el heráldico gato del aeda, tan manoseado por los críticos. El de esta piedra hurgó más hondamente y eligió el murciélago, ese binomio zoológico—entre mamífero y pájaro—, esa imagen ética—entre luzbel y ángel—, que tan bien encarna el espíritu de Baudelaire. Porque el autor de *Las flores del mal* no fue el diabolismo, en el sentido católico de este vocablo, sino un diabolismo laico y simplemente humano, un natural coeficiente de rebelión y de inocencia. La rebelión no es posible sin la inocencia. Se rebelan solamente los niños y los ángeles. La malicia no se rebela nunca. Un viejo puede únicamente despecharse y amargarse. Tal Voltaire. La rebelión es fruto del espíritu inocente. Y el gato lleva la malicia en todas sus patas. En cambio, el murciélago—ese ratón alado de las bóvedas, esa híbrida pieza de plafones—tiene el instinto de la altura y, al mismo tiempo, el de la sombra. Es natural del reino tenebroso y, a la vez, habitante de las cúpulas. Por su doble naturaleza de vuelo y de tiniebla, posee la sabiduría en la sombra y, como en los heroísmos, practica la caída para arriba.

THE MONUMENT TO BAUDELAIRE...

The monument to Baudelaire is one of the most beautiful headstones in Paris, an authentic cathedral tombstone. The sculptor took a lapidary block, split it in two and fashioned a compass. Such is the frame of the monument. A compass. An airplane, one of whose wings drags on the ground, due to its great size, just like the symbolic albatross. The other half is raised perpendicularly to the first and presents in its upper half a giant bat with outstretched wings. Above this creature, alive and floating, there is a gargoyle, whose jutting, vigilant and aggressive chin rests and does not rest upon its hands.

Another sculptor might have chiseled the heraldic cat of the bard, so groped by the critics. He, who worked this stone, however, delved deeper and chose the bat, this zoological binomial—between mammal and bird—that ethical image—between Lucifer and angel—who embodies the spirit of Baudelaire so well. And this, because the author of *The Flowers of Evil* was not diabolical, in the Catholic sense of the word, but diabolical in a lay and simply human sense, a natural coefficient of rebellion and innocence. Rebellion is not possible without innocence. Only children and angels rebel. Malice never rebels. An old man can only become spiteful and grow bitter. Hence, Voltaire. Rebellion is the fruit of an innocent spirit. And the cat carries malice in each of its paws. On the other hand, the bat—that airborne mouse of the mausoleums, that hybrid specimen of the cornices—has a knack for height and the shadows. It is a native of the kingdom of darkness and also a dweller of the cupolas. Due to its dual nature of flight and darkness, it possesses wisdom in shadows and, as in heroic acts, performs the upward fall.

CONCURRENCIA CAPITALISTA
Y EMULACIÓN SOCIALISTA

¡Quién vuela más lejos! ¿Quién da mejores puñetazos! ¡Quién nada más! ¡Quién bate el *record* de velocidad, de duración, de altura, de peso, de resistencia, de intensidad! ¡Quién hace más dinero! ¡Quién danza más! *Record* de ayuno, de canto, de risa, de matrimonios, de divorcios, de asesinatos, etc.

Este es el criterio capitalista de todo progreso.

El espíritu de *match* y de *record* nos viene del taylorismo, por el deporte, y, lógicamente, ofrece los mismos vicios y contradicciones del sistema capitalista de la concurrencia en general. Ya nadie hace nada sin mirar al rival. El hombre se mueve por cotejo con el hombre. Es una justa, no ya de fuerzas que se oponen francamente, que sería más noble y humano, sino de fuerzas que se comparan y rivalizan, que es necio, artificioso y antivital.[1] El hombre no puede ya avanzar por su propia cuenta y mirando de frente, como lo quiere el orden paralelo y multitudinario de las cosas, sino que vive y se desenvuelve teniendo en cuenta el avance y la vida de su vecino, es decir, mirando individualmente el horizonte.

Muerto el capitalismo e instaurado el socialismo, el hombre cesará de vivir comparándose con los otros, para vencerlos. El hombre vivirá entonces, solidarizándose y, a lo sumo, refiriéndose emulativa y concéntricamente a los demás. No buscará batir ningún *record*. Buscará el triunfo libre y universal de la vida.

Al régimen de la concurrencia capitalista, sucederá el régimen de la emulación socialista.

CAPITALIST COMPETITION
AND SOCIALIST EMULATION

Who flies further! Who throws better punches? Who swims the most? Who breaks the record for speed, for length, for height, for weight, for resistance, for intensity! Who makes more money! Who dances more! The record for fasting, for singing, for laughing, for marriages, for divorces, for murders, etc.

This is the capitalist criteria of Progress.

The spirit of the match and the record comes to us from Taylorism, via sports, and, logically, it offers the same vices and contradictions of the capitalist system of competition. No one does anything anymore without looking at his rival. Man moves by comparison with man. It is a joust, though not of forces that directly oppose each other, which would be more noble and human, but of forces that are compared and rivaled, and this is asinine, artificial and anti-vital. Man can no longer move forward on his own while looking ahead, as the parallel and myriad order would have it, but rather he lives and develops with the advancement and life of his neighbor in mind, that is, looking individually at the horizon.

Once Capitalism has died and Socialism taken over, man will cease to live by comparing himself to others, in order to defeat them. Man will live then, in relation to others supporting and emulating them. He will not try to break any records. He will seek the free and universal triumph of life.

The regime of capitalist competition will be overtaken by the regime of socialist emulation.

Cuando un órgano ejerce su función con plenitud, no hay malicia posible en el cuerpo. En el momento en que el tenista lanza magistralmente su bola, le posee una inocencia totalmente animal.

Lo mismo ocurre con el cerebro. En el momento en que el filósofo sorprende una nueva verdad, es una bestia completa. Anatole France decía que el sentimiento religioso es la función de un órgano especial del cuerpo humano, hasta ahora desconocido. Podría también afirmarse que, en el momento preciso en que este órgano de la fe funciona con plenitud, el creyente es también un ser desprovisto a tal punto de malicia que se diría un perfecto animal.

FROM FEUERBACH TO MARX

When an organ carries out its function fully, there is no possible malice in the body. At the moment a tennis player masterfully tosses the ball, he is possessed by animal innocence.

The same occurs with the brain. At the moment the philosopher discovers a new truth, he is a complete beast. Anatole France said that religious sentiment is the function of a special organ of the human body, yet to be discovered. One could also affirm that, at the precise moment that this organ of faith functions at its peak, the believer is also a being so devoid of malice that he could be called utterly animal.

EXPLICACIÓN DE LA HISTORIA

Hay gentes a quienes les interesan Roma, Atenas, Florencia, Toledo y otras ciudades antiguas, no por su pasado —que es lo estático e inmóvil—, sino por su actualidad —que es movimiento viviente e incesante. Para estas gentes, la obra del Greco, los mantos verdes y amarillos de sus apóstoles, su casa, su cocina, su vajilla, no interesan mayormente. ¡Qué les importa la catedral primada de Toledo con sus cinco puertas, sus siete siglos, sus frescos claustrales, su coro de plata y su encantada capilla mozárabe? ¡Qué más les da la Posada de la Sangre, donde Cervantes escribiera *La ilustre fregona*...? ¡Qué les interesa el Alcázar de Carlos V, todo de piedra y su egregio artesonado? Ya puede desaparecer en el día el célebre Castillo de San Servando, al otro lado del Tajo. Ya pueden desaparecer también los sepulcros de los héroes y cardenales de la catedral. La fábrica de armas de Toledo, ¡qué les importa...? La fina mezquita del Tránsito, construida en el siglo XIV por el judío Samuel Levi, ¡qué más les da...? La historia en texto, en leyenda, en pintura, en arquitectura, en tradición, les deja a tales transeúntes en la más completa indiferencia.

Mientras el guía les explica en el Puente de Alcántara, la fecha y circunstancias políticas de su construcción, he aquí que uno de los turistas se vuelve como escolar desaplicado y se queda viendo a un viejo toledano, que a la sazón entra, montado en un burro, a su casa. El viejo se apea trabajosamente, en mitad de su sala de recibo. ¡Ah...! —bufa el viejo y empieza a llamar a voces al guardia de la esquina, para que le ayude a desensillar el burro. Esto sucede en la calle que lleva por nombre *Travesía del horno de los bizcochos* o en aquella otra, un poco más ardua, que se llama *Bajada al Corral de Don Pedro*.

Estas escenas son las que interesan a ciertas gentes: la actualidad histórica de Toledo y no su pasado. Quieren sumergirse en la actualidad viajera, que a la postre, es la refundición y cristalización esencial de la historia pasada. Ese viejo, montado en su burro, resume en su bufido al Greco, la Catedral, el Alcázar, la Mezquita, la Fábrica de Armas. Es una escena viva y transitoria del momento, que sintetiza, como una flor, los hondos fragores y faenas difuntas de Toledo.

Lo mismo puede afirmarse de todas las ciudades antiguas, ruinas y tesoros históricos del mundo. La historia no se narra ni se mira ni se escucha ni se toca. La historia se vive y se siente vivir.

EXPLANATION OF HISTORY

There are people who are interested in Rome, Athens, Florence, Toledo and other ancient cities, not because of their past—static and immobile——but because of their present—lively and dynamic. For these people, the world of El Greco, the green and yellow robes of his apostles, his house, his kitchen, his crockery, are not very interesting. What do they care about the cathedral of Toledo, with its five doors, its seven centuries, its refreshing cloisters, its silver choir and its enchanting Mozarab chapel? What do they care about the Inn of Blood, where Cervantes was to write *The Illustrious Kitchen Maid*...? What do they care about the Palace of Carlos V, all of its stone and its distinguished coffered ceiling? The celebrated Castle of San Servando on the other side of the ravine might as well disappear in broad daylight. The tombs of the heroes and cardinals of the cathedral might as well disappear. The Munitions Factory in Toledo—what do they care!? The Tránsito Mosque, constructed in the XIV century by the Jew Samuel Levi—what do they care!? These passersby are utterly indifferent to history in a text, in a legend, in a painting, in architecture, in tradition.

While the guide explains the date and political circumstances of its construction on the Bridge of Alcántara, I note that one of the tourists becomes a disengaged schoolboy and stares at an old Toledan, who is just arriving home on the back of his donkey. The old man laboriously gets down, in the middle of his receiving room. "Ah...!" the old man snorts and begins to loudly call to the watchmen on the corner, so that they help him remove the donkey's saddle. This happens on the street that bears the name *Sponge Cake Oven Way* or on that slightly rougher one called *Don Pedro's Path to the Chicken Coop*.

These are the scenes that interest certain people: the historical present of Toledo; not its past. They want to submerge in the fleeting present, which in the end recasts and crystallizes the essentials of past history. That old man, seated atop a donkey, summarizes in his snort El Greco, the Cathedral, the Palace, the Mosque, the Munitions Factory. It is a living and transitory scene of the moment, synthesizing, like a flower, Toledo's uproar and defunct deeds.

The same can be said of all the ancient cities, historical ruins and treasures of the world. One does not narrate history, or see it or hear it or touch it. One lives history and feels it live.

AL ANIMAL SE LE GUIA...

Al animal se le guía o se le empuja. Al hombre se le acompaña paralelamente.

EXISTEN PREGUNTAS...

Existen preguntas sin respuestas, que son el espíritu de la ciencia y el sentido común hecho inquietud. Existen respuestas sin preguntas, que son el espíritu del arte y la conciencia dialéctica de las cosas.

LA CABEZA Y LOS PIES DE LA DIALÉCTICA

Ante las piedras de riesgo darwineano, de que están construidos los palacios de las Tullerías, de Potsdam, de Peterhof, el Quirinal, la Casa Blanca y el Buckingham, sufro la pena de un megaterio, que meditase parado, las patas traseras sobre la cabeza de Hegel y las delanteras sobre la cabeza de Marx.

LA MUERTE DE LA MUERTE

En realidad, el cielo no queda lejos ni cerca de la tierra. En realidad, la muerte no queda cerca ni lejos de la vida. Estamos siempre ante el río de Heráclito.

AN ANIMAL IS LED...

An animal is led or is pushed. Man is accompanied in parallel.

THERE EXIST QUESTIONS...

There exist questions without answers, which fill the spirit of science and common sense with uneasiness. There exist answers without questions, which are the spirit of art and the dialectic consciousness of things.

THE HEAD AND FEET OF DIALECTICS

Facing the stones of Darwinian risk that compose the Tuileries palace, Potstam, Peterhof, Quirinal, the White House and Buckingham, I suffer the pain of a megatherium, who meditated standing upright, the hind legs on the head of Hegel and the front legs on the head of Marx.

THE DEATH OF DEATH

In reality, the sky isn't far from or near the land. In reality, death isn't far from or close to life. We are always before the river of Heraclitus.

CON EL ADVENIMIENTO DEL AVIÓN...

Con el advenimiento del avión y de la telegrafía inalámbrica, el sentimiento de nostalgia de distancia va, en cierto modo, y hasta nueva orden, debilitándose o desapareciendo. Lo que no desaparece, con los progresos científicos e industriales, es la nostalgia de tiempo.

ENTRE LAS MIL O MÁS...

Entre las mil o más voces simultáneas de un coro, se oye únicamente dos de ellas.

No hay nada que temer. No hay nada que esperar. Siempre se está más o menos vivo. Siempre se está más o menos muerto.

La música viene del reloj. La música, como arte, nació en el momento en que el hombre se dio cuenta, por la vez primera, de la existencia del tiempo, digo, de la marcha de las cosas, del movimiento universal. ¡Uno! ¡Dos...! Y la escala nació.

WITH THE ADVENT OF THE AIRPLANE...

With the advent of the airplane and wireless telegraph, the nostalgic feeling of distance continues, by some means, unto a new order, growing weak or disappearing. What doesn't disappear with scientific and industrial progress is the nostalgia of time.

AMONG THE THOUSAND OR MORE...

Among the thousand or more simultaneous voices of the chorus, only two are heard.

There is nothing to fear. One is always more or less alive. One is always more or less dead.

Music comes from the clock. Music, like art, was born at the moment when man, for the first time, noticed the existence of time, that is to say, the course of things, the universal movement. One! Two! And the scale was born.

EL MOVIMIENTO CONSUSTANCIAL DE LA MATERIA

Las paralelas no existen en el espíritu ni en la realidad del universo. Se trata de una mera figuración abstracta de la geometría. No cabe paralelismo dentro de la continuidad, una y lineal, de la vida. La historia y la naturaleza se desenvuelven linealmente y, en esta única línea, solitaria, los hechos humanos y los fenómenos naturales se suceden, uno tras otro, sucesiva y nunca simultáneamente.

El paralelismo de una línea férrea no tiene mayor realidad viviente que el de dos líneas que se trazan en una pizarra. Dos árboles o dos niños que nacen en un mismo instante, tampoco constituyen un paralelismo efectivo. En todos estos casos la ilusión geométrica no se sustenta en hechos objetivos, sino que participa de la naturaleza de otras tantas ficciones de los sentidos o abstracciones de la inteligencia, como cuando se ve, desde un tren en marcha, que las casas desfilan o cuando, moviendo circularmente un tizón encendido (véase Pascal), creemos ver y constatar un arco de fuego, etc.

La vida es una sucesión y no una simultaneidad. Las paralelas aparentes de una línea férrea, no se desarrollan a la vez, sino una después de otra. Los hombres no conviven, sino que se suceden de uno en uno. Los pueblos tampoco conviven sino que se suceden. La pluralidad es un fenómeno del tiempo y no del espacio. El número 1 está solitario de lugar. El 2 y los guarismos subsiguientes, dígitos o compuestos, no existen como realidad objetiva, sino como figuraciones abstractas del pensamiento.

La vida no se ensaya en varias formas a la vez. Sino en varias formas sucesivas. Un planeta no tiene un destino diverso al de los otros planetas, sino el mismo y único fin que los otros no han podido realizar. Una piedra ensaya un idéntico destino que un molusco y ella marcha antes o después de un hombre, pero no al mismo tiempo que él. Si se pudiera figurar la evolución de la vida, se la representaría por una fila de seres y de cosas, de uno en fondo. En el terreno abstracto, los seres y las cosas se desenvuelven con un aparente carácter multitudinario. Pero, esto no es la realidad substantiva. Bajo la ilusoria simultaneidad de las cosas y los seres, reposa, en el fondo, la realidad exclusivamente sucesiva y en marcha del universo. La masa es más un desfile que un remolino. La asíntota surgente de la historia tiene más de línea que de punto.

THE INTRINSIC MOVEMENT OF MATTER

Parallels exist neither in the spirit nor in the reality of the universe. It is but an abstract supposition of geometry. There is no room for a parallelism within the single and linear continuity of life. History and nature unfold linearly and, in this single, solitary line, human events and natural phenomena occur, one after another, successively and never simultaneously.

The parallelism of a railroad does not have a greater living reality than that of two lines drawn on a chalkboard. Two trees or two children born at the same instant do not constitute an effective parallelism either. In all these cases, the geometrical illusion does not sustain objective events, but participates in the nature of so many other fictions of the senses or abstractions of intelligence, like when we see, from a train in motion, that the houses are on parade or when, a burning stick is moving in a circle (see Pascal), we believe that we see and affirm an arc of fire, etc.

Life is a succession and not simultaneity. The apparent parallels of a railroad do not develop at once, but one after another. Men do not live together, but they occur one after another. Towns do not live together either, but occur. Plurality is a phenomenon of time and not of space. The number 1 is solitary of place. The number 2 and the subsequent single or compound numbers do not exist as objective reality, but as abstract suppositions of thought.

Life does not transpire in various forms at once. But in various successive forms. A planet does not have a destiny different from that of other planets, but the same and unique end that all the others have managed to carry out. A stone meets a destiny identical to that of a mollusk, and it goes before or after a man, but not at the same time as he. If one could depict the evolution of life, it would be represented by a line of beings and things, with one at the end. In abstract terrain, beings and things unfold with an apparent myriad character. But this is not substantive reality. Beneath the illusory simultaneity of things and beings, reality, at the end, is solely a succession in the movement of the universe. The masses are more a parade than a crowd. The asyndeton surging from history is more a line than a point.

INDIVIDUO Y SOCIEDAD

Cuando se inició el interrogatorio, el asesino dio su primera respuesta, dirigiendo una larga mirada sobre los miembros del Tribunal. Uno de éstos, el sustituto Milad, ofrecía un parecido asombroso con el acusado. La misma edad, el mismo ojo derecho mutilado, el corte y color del bigote, la línea y espesor del busto, la forma de la cabeza, el peinado. Un doble absolutamente idéntico. El asesino vio a su doble y algo debió acontecer en su conciencia. Hizo girar extrañamente su ojo izquierdo y muerto, extrajo su pañuelo y enjugó el sudor de sus duras mejillas. La primera pregunta de fondo, formulada por el presidente del Tribunal, decía:

—A usted le gustaban las mujeres y, además de Malou, tuvo usted a su doméstica, a su cuñada y dos queridas más...

El acusado comprendió el alcance procesal de esta pregunta. Confuso, fue a clavar su único ojo bueno en el sustituto Milad, su doble, y dijo:

—Me gustaban las mujeres, como gustan a todos los hombres...

El asesino parecía sentir un nudo en la garganta. La presencia de su doble empezaba a causar en él un visible aunque misterioso malestar, un gran miedo acaso... Siempre que se le formulaba una pregunta grave y tremenda, miraba con su único ojo a su doble y respondía cada vez más vencido. La presencia de Milad le hacía un daño creciente, influyendo funestamente en la marcha de su espíritu y del juicio. Al final de la primera audiencia, sacó su pañuelo y se puso a llorar.

En la tarde de la segunda audiencia, se ha mostrado aún más abatido. Ayer, día de la sentencia, el asesino era, antes de la condena, un guiñapo de hombre, un deshecho, un culpable irremediablemente perdido. Casi no ha hablado ya. Al leerse el veredicto de muerte, estuvo hundido en su banco, la cabeza sumersa entre las manos, insensible, frío, como una piedra. Cuando en medio del alboroto y los murmullos de la multitud consternada, le sacaron los guardias, solo miraba fijamente a la cara de Milad, su doble, el sustituto.

A tal punto es social y solidaria la conciencia individual.

INDIVIDUAL AND SOCIETY

When the interrogation began, the murderer gave his first answer, staring at the members of the Tribunal. One of these, Milad the substitute, bore an astonishing likeness to the defendant. The same age, the same mutilated right eye, the cut and color of the mustache, the line and thickness of his chest, the shape of his head, the hair cut. An absolutely identical double. The murderer saw his double and something must have happened in his conscience. He made his left and dead eye turn in a strange way, took out a handkerchief and wiped the sweat from his hard cheeks. The first background question, formulated by the president of the panel, was this:

"You, sir, took a liking to women and, aside from Malou, you had your maid, your sister-in-law and two other lovers..."

The defendant comprehended the procedural scope of this question. Poker-faced, he fixed his only good eye on Milad the substitute, his double, and he said:

"I took a liking to women, as all men take a liking to them..."

The murderer seemed to feel a knot in his throat. The presence of his double began to cause in him a visible yet mysterious discomfort, a great fear perhaps... Every time a serious and terrible question was formulated, he stared with his only eye at his double and responded each time more defeated. The presence of Milad caused him greater and greater pain, disastrously influencing the course of his spirit and of the trial. At the end of the first hearing, he took out his handkerchief and burst into tears.

On the afternoon of the second hearing, he looked even more dejected. Yesterday, the day of the sentence, the murderer was, before his sentence, a wreck of a man, devastated, a hopelessly lost culprit. He barely even spoke anymore. As the verdict of death was being read, he was slouching in his chair, his head resting on his hands, numb, cold, like a stone. When the bailiffs took him away, amid the clamor and murmuring of the dismayed crowd, he only fixed his gaze on the face of Milad, his double, the substitute.

To that extent the individual conscience is social and collective.

SIN MOSTRAR EL MENOR SIGNO DE TEMOR...

Sin mostrar el menor signo de temor, ni siquiera disfrazarse, el asesino siguió viviendo normalmente, a la vista general. Lejos de esconderse, como lo habría hecho cualquier matador ramplón, anduvo por todas partes. La policía no pudo encontrarle, precisamente porque él no se escondió. Pascal ha tenido razón, cuando ha dicho: «Tú no me buscarías, si no me hubieras ya encontrado».

A tal punto el individual es libre e independiente de la sociedad.

EXPLICACIÓN DEL EJÉRCITO ROJO

Un hombre cuyo nivel de cultura —hablo de la cultura basada en la idea y la práctica de la justicia, que es la única cultura verdadera— un hombre, digo, cuyo nivel de cultura está por debajo del esfuerzo creador que supone la invención de un fusil, no tiene derecho de usarlo.

WITHOUT SHOWING THE LEAST SIGN OF FEAR...

Without showing the least sign of fear, nor even masking himself, the murderer kept on living normally, in the public eye. Far from hiding, as any vulgar murderer would have done, he went about everywhere. The police couldn't find him, precisely because he wasn't hiding. Pascal was right, when he said: "You would not look for me, had you not already found me."

To this extent the individual is free and independent of society.

EXPLANATION OF THE RED ARMY

A man whose level of culture—I'm talking about culture based on the idea and practice of justice, which is the only true culture—a man, I was saying, whose level of culture is driven by the creative force that gives rise to the invention of a rifle, this man does not have the right to use it.

NEGACIONES DE NEGACIONES

André Bretón cuenta que Philippe Soupault salió una mañana de su casa y se echó a recorrer París, preguntando de puerta en puerta:

—¿Aquí vive el señor Philippe Soupault?

Después de atravesar varias calles, de una casa desconocida salieron a responderle:

—Sí, señor, aquí vive el señor Philippe Soupault.

-:-:-:-:-

Un detective que figura en una novela de Chesterton, empeñado en encontrar el lugar donde se ocultaba un criminal, dio con él, guiado y atraído por ciertos detalles raros que ofrecía, en su arquitectura, la casa donde estaba escondido el delincuente.

-:-:-:-:-

Un día que salía yo del Louvre, a un amigo que encontré en la puerta del museo y que me preguntó adónde iba, le dije:

—Al Museo del Louvre.

-:-:-:-:-

Bueno sería recordar que Colón, según relata el biógrafo André de Loffechi, tuvo por la primera vez el sentimiento de la redondez del globo entrando a su dormitorio, en Génova. «Si en lugar de entrar a su dormitorio —observa Loffechi— sale Colón al jardín, pongamos por caso, no habría seguramente descubierto América».

-:-:-:-:-

Marquet de Vasselot se valió, sin darse cuenta, de una voltereta en su cama para descubrir el principio científico según el cual algunos bronces chinos de la época de la dinastía de Sing, mantienen una coloración azulada al contacto del aire.

-:-:-:-:-

NEGATIONS OF NEGATIONS

André Bretón says that Philippe Soupault left his house one morning and began running all over Paris, asking from door to door:

"Does Mr. Philippe Soupault live here?"

After going through various streets, at an unknown house they answered the door and said:

"Yes, sir, Mr. Philippe Soupault lives here."

-:-:-:-:-

A detective who appears in a Chesterton novel, bent on finding the place where the criminal was hiding, discovered him, guided and attracted by certain odd details in the architecture of the house where the criminal was hiding.

-:-:-:-:-

One day when I was coming out of the Louvre, I ran into a friend at the door to the museum who asked me where I was going. I said:
"To the Louvre Museum."

-:-:-:-:-

It would be good to remember that Columbus, as biographer André de Loffechi tells us, experienced his first feeling of the earth's roundness as he was entering his bedroom in Genoa. "If instead of entering his bedroom," Loffechi observes, "let's say, Columbus goes out to the garden, then he would not necessarily have discovered America."

-:-:-:-:-

Marquis de Vasselot unwittingly used a somersault in his bed to discover the scientific principle by which certain Chinese bronze pieces from the Tsing dynasty period maintain a bluish coloring when in contact with the air.

-:-:-:-:-

Lord Carnavon, que descubrió en febrero 1923 el tercer hipogeo funerario de Tut-Ankh-Amon, padecía, según se ha sabido después de su muerte, de una misteriosa enfermedad nerviosa. Su compañero de aventura arqueológica, Mr. Howard Carter, refiere que el infortunado Lord, estando aún en Londres, antes de su hallazgo faraónico, cada vez que venía a sus narices un olor a resina, sin saber por qué, se ponía mal y le acometían cavilaciones melancólicas. Entraba entonces a su biblioteca y abría sus volúmenes. El propio Mr. Howard Carter, al encontrar el sarcófago de oro macizo en que estaba encerrada la momia de Tut-Ankh-Amon, el héroe buscado por Carnavon, ha constatado que dicha momia se hallaba cubierta de una espesa capa de resina sagrada.

-:-:-:-:-

Los trescientos estados de mujer de la Tour Eiffel, están helados. La herzciana crin de cultura de la torre, su pelusa de miras, su vivo aceraje, engrapado al sistema moral de Descartes, están helados.

Le Bois de Boulogne, verde por cláusula privada, está helado.

La Cámara de Diputados, donde Briand clama: «Hago un llamamiento a los pueblos de la tierra...», y a cuyas puertas el centinela acaricia, sin darse cuenta, su cápsula de humanas inquietudes, su simple bomba de hombre, su eterno principio de Pascal, está helada.

Los Campos Elíseos, grises por cláusula pública, están helados.

Las estatuas que periplan[2] la Plaza de la Concordia y sobre cuyos gorros frigios se oye al tiempo estudiar para infinito, están heladas.

Los dados de los calvarios católicos de París, están helados hasta por la cara de los treses.

Los gallos civiles, suspensos en las agujas góticas de Nôtre-Dame y del Sacré Cœur, están helados.

La doncella de las campiñas de París, cuyo pulgar no se repite nunca al medir el alcance de sus ojos, está helada.

El andante a dos rumbos de *El pájaro de fuego* de Stravinsky, está helado.

Los garabatos escritos por Einstein en la pizarra del anfiteatro Richelieu de la Sorbona, están helados.

Los billetes de avión para el viaje de París a Buenos Aires, en dos horas, 23 minutos, 8 segundos, están helados.

El sol está helado.

El fuego central de la tierra está helado.

El padre, meridiano, y el hijo, paralelo, están helados.

Las dos desviaciones de la historia están heladas.

Lord Carnavon, who in February of 1923 discovered the third underground funeral tomb of Tut-Ankh-Amon, suffered, according to what has been learned after his death, from a mysterious nervous illness. His companion in archeological adventure, Mr. Howard Carter, tells us that the unfortunate Lord, while still in London before his pharaonic finding, without knowing why, would become ill and would be struck by melancholic thoughts each time the scent of resin reached his nose. He then would enter his library and open up his volumes. After finding the object of Carnavon's search, the gold sarcophagus of the Tut-Ankh-Amon's mummy, Mr. Carter has stated that said mummy was found covered with a thick layer of sacred resin.

-:-:-:-:-

The Eiffel Tower's three hundred womanly states are frozen. The tower's Hertzian mane of culture, its fuzzy sights, its living steelwork, stapled to Descartes' moral system, is frozen.

Le Bois de Boulogne, green from a private clause, is frozen.

The Chamber of Deputies, where Briand exclaims: "I hereby appeal to the peoples of the land" while the doorkeeper unconsciously caresses, his capsule of human uneasiness, his simple pump of Man, according to Pascal's principle, it is frozen.

The Elysian Fields, gray from a public clause, are frozen.

The statues that circuit the Place de la Concorde upon whose Phrygian caps time is heard studying the infinite, they are frozen.

The dice of the Catholic cavalries of Paris are even frozen on the face of the threes.

The civil cocks, suspended in the gothic needles of Nôtre-Dame and of Sacré Cœur, are frozen.

The maiden of the Parisian countryside, whose thumb measures the horizon with her eyes only once, is frozen.

The two textured andante in Stravinsky's *The Firebird* is frozen.

Einstein's scribbles on the chalkboard of the Richelieu amphitheater at the Sorbonne are frozen.

The airline tickets for the trip from Paris to Buenos Aires, in 2 hours, 23 minutes, 8 seconds, are frozen.

The sun is frozen.

The fire at the earth's core is frozen.

The father, meridian, and the son, parallel, are frozen.

History's two deviations are frozen.

Mi acto menor de hombre está helado.
Mi oscilación sexual está helada.

-:-:-:-:-

Quiero perderme por falta de caminos. Siento el ansia de perderme definitivamente, no ya en el mundo ni en la moral, sino en la vida y por obra de la vida. Odio las calles y los senderos, que no permiten perderse. La ciudad y el campo son así. No es posible en ellos la pérdida, que no la perdición, de un espíritu. En el campo y en la ciudad, se está demasiado asistido de rutas, flechas y señales, para poder perderse. Uno está allí indefectiblemente limitado, al norte, al sur, al este, al oeste. Uno está allí irremediablemente situado. Al revés de lo que le ocurrió a Wilde, la mañana en que iba a morir en París, a mí me ocurre en la ciudad amanecer siempre rodeado de todo, del peine, de la pastilla de jabón, de todo. Amanezco en el mundo y con el mundo, en mí mismo y conmigo mismo. Llamo e inevitablemente me contestan y se oye mi llamada. Salgo a la calle y hay calle. Me echo a pensar y hay siempre pensamiento. Esto es desesperante.

-:-:-:-:-

Los técnicos hablan y viven como técnicos y rara vez como hombres. Es muy difícil ser técnico y hombre, al mismo tiempo. Un poeta juzga un poema, no como simple mortal, sino como poeta. Y ya sabemos hasta qué punto los técnicos se enredan en los hilos de los bastidores, cayendo por el lado flaco del sistema, del prejuicio doctrinario o del interés profesional, consciente o subconsciente y fracturándose así la sensibilidad plena del hombre.

-:-:-:-:-

Todas las cosas llevan su sombrero. Todos los animales llevan su sombrero. Los vegetales llevan también el suyo. No hay en este mundo nada ni nadie que no lleve la cabeza cubierta. Aunque los hombres se quiten el sombrero, siempre queda la cabeza cubierta de algo que podríamos llamar el sombrero innato, natural y tácito de cada persona.

Desde el punto de vista del hombre, los sombreros se clasifican en sombreros naturales y sombreros artificiales. Se llama sombrero natural aquel que nace con cada persona y que le es inseparable aún después de

My minor act of man is frozen.
My sexual oscillation is frozen.

-:-:-:-:-

I want to get lost from a lack of roads. I'm itching to get lost permanent-
ly, no longer in the world nor in morality, but in life and by dint of life. I
hate the streets and paths that don't allow one to get lost. The city and
country are like this. In them, the loss, though not the perdition of a spir-
it, is impossible. In the country and in the city, one is far too surrounded
by routes, arrows and signs, to get lost. One is without fail limited there,
to the north, to the south, to the east, to the west. One is inevitably situ-
ated there. Contrary to what happened to Wilde, on the morning he was
to die in Paris, I always awake in the city surrounded by everything, by
the brush, by the bar of soap, by everything. I awake in the world and
with the world, in myself and with myself. I call and inevitably they
answer, and my call is heard. I go out onto the street, and there is a street.
I starting thinking, and there always is thought. This is exasperating.

-:-:-:-:-

Technicians speak and live as technicians and rarely as men. It is quite
difficult to be a technician and a man at the same time. A poet judges a
poem, not as a simple mortal, but as a poet. And we already know to
what extent technicians get tangled up offstage in the fly ropes, falling
through the weak side of the system, from indoctrinating prejudice or
from professional interest, conscious or subconscious, and in this way
fracturing the complete sensibility of man.

-:-:-:-:-

Every thing wears its hat. All animals wear their hats. The plants wear
theirs as well. There is not in this world anything or anyone that doesn't
cover their heads. Even though men may remove their hats, the head
always stays covered by something we could call the innate, natural and
tacit hat of each person.
    From man's point of view, hats are classified as natural hats and arti-
ficial hats. We call a natural hat one that is born with each person and is
inseparable from him even in death. In the skeleton, the presence of the

la muerte. En el esqueleto, la presencia del sombrero natural y tácito es palpable. Se llama sombrero artificial aquel que se adquiere en las sombrererías y del cual podemos separarnos momentánea o eternamente. En el esqueleto, la falta de este sombrero artificial es, asimismo, evidente.

-:-:-:-:-

Se rechaza las cosas que andan lado a lado del camino y no en él. ¡Ay del que engendra un monstruo! ¡Ay del que irradia un arco recto! ¡Ay del que logra cristalizar un gran disparate! Crucificados en vanas camisas de fuerza, avanzan así las diferencias de hojas alternas hacia el Panteón de los grandes acordes.

-:-:-:-:-

Conozco a un hombre que dormía con sus brazos. Un día se los amputaron y quedó despierto para siempre.

-:-:-:-:-

El agua invita a la meditación. La tierra, a la acción. La meditación es hidrográfica; la acción geográfica. La meditación viene. La acción va. Aquélla es centrípeta; ésta, centrífuga.

-:-:-:-:-

La danza, al repetirse, se estereotipa y se torna cliché. Cada danza debe ser improvisada y morir en seguida. Esto hacen los negros.

-:-:-:-:-

Si no se quiere que el teatro, como representación, desaparezca, convendría, al menos, que cada pieza sea improvisada —texto, decorado, movimiento escénico— por los actores mismos, que, al efecto, deben ser también autores y *régisseurs* de las obras que representan. Tal hace Chaplin en la pantalla.

-:-:-:-:-

natural and tacit hat is palpable. We call an artificial hat one that is acquired in hat shops and from which we can separate ourselves momentarily or eternally. In the skeleton, the lack of this artificial hat is, likewise, evident.

-:-:-:-:-

Those who take to the shoulder and not to the road itself will be rejected. Woe betide he who spawns a monster! Woe betide he who radiates a strait arc! Woe betide he who manages to crystallize some utter nonsense! This is how the differences of distichous leaves march on the Pantheon of the big deals, crucified in useless straitjackets.

-:-:-:-:-

I know a man who used to sleep with his arms. One day they amputated them and he stayed awake forever.

-:-:-:-:-

Water invites meditation. Land, action. Meditation is hydrographic; action, geographic. Meditation comes. Action goes. That one is a centripetal; this one, centrifugal.

-:-:-:-:-

Dance, when repeated, gets stereotyped and becomes cliché. Each dance should be improvised and die shortly thereafter. This is how the Negroes do it.

-:-:-:-:-

If one does not want theater, as a performance, to disappear, it would be good, at least, for each component—text, scene, movement—to be improved by the actors themselves, who, in effect, should also be authors and *régisseurs* of the works that they act out. This is what Chaplin does on the silver screen.

-:-:-:-:-

Un médico afirma que para fruncir el entrecejo, se necesita poner en juego sesenta y cuatro músculos, mientras que para reír son suficientes trece músculos. El dolor es, por consiguiente, más deportivo que la alegría.

-:-:-:-:-

Las personas y cosas que se cruzan en opuestas direcciones, no van a sitios diferentes. Todos van al mismo sitio, sólo que van una tras de otra.

-:-:-:-:-

Los que viajan en la proa, llevan la izquierda de las cosas; los que viajan en la popa, el centro. La derecha de las cosas la lleva el piloto.

-:-:-:-:-

La idea es la historia del acto y, naturalmente, posterior a él. Primero se vive un acto y, luego, éste queda troquelado en una idea, la suya correspondiente. Paul Valéry me excusará este pequeño aterrizaje, esta conjugación del infinitivo de *El alma y la danza*.

-:-:-:-:-

Se está siempre tomando el cuchillo por la punta, en lugar de tomarlo por el mango. Hay hombres destinados a engendrar genios y los hay destinados a hacer obras geniales. El coito en que el padre de Dostoiewski engendró al gran novelista, vale tanto como *El idiota*. Entre una y otra cosa yace un reloj encadenado.

-:-:-:-:-

El día tiene a la noche encerrada adentro. La noche tiene al día encerrado afuera.

-:-:-:-:-

Le vi pasar tan rápido, que no le vi.

-:-:-:-:-

A doctor affirms that in order to furrow the brow, one must flex sixty-four muscles, while in order to laugh thirteen muscles are sufficient. Pain, therefore, is more athletic than joy.

-:-:-:-:-

People and things that cross each other in opposite directions don't go to different places. They all go to the same place; it's just that they go one after the other.

-:-:-:-:-

Those who travel on the bow carry the port side; those who travel on the stern, the center. The starboard side, the skipper's got that.

-:-:-:-:-

The idea is the history of the act and, naturally, posterior to it. First one lives an act and, then, this act is minted into an idea, its correlate. Paul Valéry will have to excuse this small landing, this conjugation of the infinitive of *Dance and the Soul*.

-:-:-:-:-

The knife is always being taken by the blade instead of being taken by the handle. There are men destined to engender geniuses and there are others destined to create works of genius. The coitus in which Dostoevsky's father engendered the great novelist is worth as much as the *The Idiot*. Between one thing and another there lies a chained clock.

-:-:-:-:-

The day has the night locked inside. The night has the day locked outside.

-:-:-:-:-

I saw him pass by so quickly that I didn't see him.

-:-:-:-:-

En un match de velocidad entre una bicicleta y una rana, ¿quién saldrá ganando? La rana, —diría Averchenko.

-:-:-:-:-

Estuve lejos de mi padre doscientos años y me escribían que él vivía siempre. Pero un sentimiento profundo de la vida, me daba la necesidad entrañable y creadora de creerle muerto.

-:-:-:-:-

Renan decía de Joseph de Maistre: «Cada vez que en su obra hay un efecto de estilo, ello es debido a una falta de francés». Lo mismo puede decirse de todos los grandes escritores de los diversos idiomas.

-:-:-:-:-

Se puede hablar de freno sólo cuando se trata de la actividad cerebral, que tiene el suyo en la razón. El sentimiento no se desboca nunca. Tiene su medida en sí mismo y la proporción en su propia naturaleza. El sentimiento está siempre de buen tamaño. Nunca es deficiente ni excesivo. No necesita de brida ni de espuelas.

-:-:-:-:-

El ruido de un carro, cuando éste va lentamente, es feo y desagradable. Cuando va rápidamente, se torna melodioso.

Who will win a race between a bicycle and a frog? Averchenko would say, the frog.

-:-:-:-

I was far from my father for two hundred years and they wrote to me saying that he was still living. But a profound feeling from life gave me the deep and creative need to believe that he was dead.

-:-:-:-

Renan said of Joseph de Maistre: "Every time that there is an effect of style in his work, it is due to a lack of French." The same can be said of all the great writers in all the different languages.

-:-:-:-

One can speak of the horse's bit only when dealing with cerebral activity, founded on reason. Feeling is never in excess. It has its measure in itself and proportion in its own nature. Feeling is always the right size. It's never deficient or excessive. It needs neither a bridle nor spurs.

-:-:-:-

The noise of a car, when it goes slowly, is ugly and unpleasant. When it goes quickly, it becomes melodious.

TEORÍA DE LA REPUTACIÓN

He estado en la famosa taberna *Sztaron* de la calle de Seipel, en Budapest, taberna, según se murmura, de una secreta firma bolchevique y cuyo gerente, Ossag Muchay, es tan cortés con la clientela. Muchay ha estado conmigo un gran rato, conversando y bebiendo absintio de Viena, esa distilación religiosa y armada, color de convólvulo, que extrae de una extraña gramínea salvaje, llamada *dístilo dormido*. La taberna, esta tarde, se ha visto visitada por muy contados parroquianos, que entraban, estirando los miembros, bebían malvadamente ante el mostrador y se iban con gran perfección. Dos muchachas jugaban en un rincón de la planta baja, un juego de dulce de hierro,[3] con pequeñas tortugas de capa y cintas de colores. A la entrada de la misma sala, platicábamos el buen Muchay y yo. Hablábamos de las supersticiones del Asia Menor, de las salobres ciencias de aprehensión, de las hechicerías.

Me despedí de Muchay y abandoné la taberna. Avancé hacia la esquina y tomé la calle de Praga, que apareció invadida de gente. La multitud observaba por sobre los tejados las maniobras de la policía. Enteréme, por crecidas puntuales y menguantes de viñeta, que se perseguía a un delincuente de un alto delito, que nadie sabía precisar. Un grupo de gendarmes salió de una de las torres de la iglesia de Ravulk, conduciendo preso a un hombre. Al descender el prisionero las gradas del atrio, pude verle entre la muchedumbre, trajeado de una pelliza en losanges, los ojos enormes, perrazo de gran estimación, que acabase de morder a una reina.

Hasta el comisariado fui detrás de esta gente. El comisario interrogó al preso, en tono de legal indignación:

—¿Quién es usted? ¿Cuál es su nombre?

—Yo no tengo nombre, señor, —dijo el preso.

Se ha averiguado en Loeben, aldea donde vivía el aherrojado, por su nombre, sin conseguirlo. Nadie da razón de nada que se relacione con sus antecedentes de familia. En sus bolsillos tampoco se ha sorprendido papel alguno. Lo único que está probado es que vive en Loeben, porque todo el mundo le ha viso allí a diario, caminar por las calles, sentarse en los garitos, leer periódicos, conversar con los transeúntes. Pero nadie conoce su nombre. ¿Desde cuándo vivía en Loeben? Se ignora, por otro lado, si es húngaro o extranjero.

He vuelto a la taberna de Ossag Muchay y le he referido el caso en todos sus detalles y aun dándole la filiación minuciosa del preso. Muchay me ha dicho:

REPUTATION THEORY

I have been in the famous *Sztaron* tavern on Seipel Street, in Budapest; a tavern, they say, of a secret Bolshevik company whose manager, Ossag Muchay, has been quite courteous to his clientele. Muchay has been with me for quite a while, talking at length and sipping Viennese absinth, that religious and potent liqueur, the color of an inch worm that he extracts from a strange wild grass, called *sleeping spirit*. This evening, the tavern was visited by a great number of parishioners, who entered, stretching out their limbs, drinking maliciously at the bar and then leaving with utter perfection. In the corner on the first floor, two young girls were playing a game of leap-frog with tiny caped turtles bedecked in ribbons. In the doorway of the same room, good Muchay and I were talking. We spoke about the superstitions of Asia Minor, about the salubrious sciences of apprehension, about witchcraft.

I said goodbye to Muchay and left the tavern. I headed toward the corner and took Prague Street, which appeared to be invaded with people. The crowd was looking over the brick walls at the police maneuvers. I realized, through timely waning swells in vignette, that they were chasing the criminal of a high crime, one which no one could identify. A group of officers left one of the towers of the Ravulk church, leading a man in handcuffs. As they led the prisoner down the steps of the entrance hall, I could see him through the crowd, wearing a coat with lozenges, enormous eyes, a large well-bred dog, who had just bitten a queen.

I followed the throng of people to the station. The commissioner himself interrogated the prisoner in a tone of legal indignation:

"Who are you? What is your name?"

"I don't have a name, sir," said the prisoner.

His name has been sought in Loeben, the village where the shackled man was residing, but to no avail. There is no official record of his family. Nor was any paper at all discovered in his pockets. All that is proven is that he lives in Loeben, because everyone has seen him there on a daily basis, walking through the streets, sitting in the cafes, reading newspapers, talking with passersby. Yet, no one knows his name. How long has he lived in Loeben? This remains unknown, as does whether he is Hungarian or a foreigner.

I returned to Ossag Muchay's tavern and explained the case to him in great detail and even gave him the minute description of the prisoner. Muchay told me:

—Ese individuo carece, en verdad, de nombre. Soy yo quien guarda su nombre. ¿Quiere usted conocerlo?

Me tomó por el brazo, subimos al segundo piso y me condujo a un escritorio. Allí extrajo de un diminuto estuche de acero un retazo de papel, donde aparecía, en trazos gruesos y resueltos, pero tan enredados que era imposible descifrarlos, una·firma delineada con tinta verde rana, de la que usan los campesinos de Hungría. Argumenté a Muchay:

—¿Se puede acaso tomar el nombre de una persona y esconderlo en un estuche, como una simple sortija o un billete...?

—Ni más ni menos, —me respondió el tabernero.

—¿Y qué explicación tiene todo esto? ¿Cuál es, en resumen, ese nombre?

—Usted ni nadie puede saberlo, pues este nombre es ahora de mi exclusiva posesión. Puede usted conocerlo, mas no saberlo...

—¿Se burla usted de mí, señor Muchay?

—De ninguna manera. Aquel hombre perdió su nombre y él mismo, aunque quisiera darlo, no puede ya saberlo. Le es absolutamente imposible, en tanto no tenga en su poder la firma que usted está viendo aquí.

—Pero si él la trazó, le será fácil trazar otra y otras.

—No. El nombre no es sino uno solo. Las firmas son muchas, sin duda, mas el nombre está en una sola de las firmas, entre todas.

Sus inesperadas sutilezas de billar, empezaron a hacerme palos. Muchay, en cambio, hablaba sin vacilaciones. Encendió su pipa con dos centellas de pedernal croata. Cerró su estuche de acero y me invitó a bajar.

—La vida de un hombre, —me dijo, descendiendo la escalera—, está revelada toda entera en uno solo de sus actos. El nombre de un hombre está revelado en una sola de sus firmas. Saber ese acto representativo, es saber su vida verdadera. Saber esa firma representativa, es saber su nombre verdadero.

—¿Y en qué se funda usted para creer que la firma que usted posee, es la firma representativa de ese hombre? Además, ¿qué importancia tiene el saber el nombre verdadero de una persona? ¿No se sabe, acaso, el nombre verdadero de todas las personas?

—¿Escuche usted, —me argumentó Muchay, dando inflexión prudente a sus palabras—, el nombre verdadero de muchas personas se ignora. Esta es la causa por la cual, en lugar de apresar al obrero de Loeben, no se ha apresado al patrón de la fábrica donde éste trabaja.

—Pero usted sabe el delito de que se le acusa?

—De un atentado contra el Regente Horthy.

"That individual, in all truth, lacks a name. I am the only one who holds his name. Do you want to find out what it is?"

He took me by the arm, we went up to the second floor and he led me to a desk. There, he took a scrap of paper out of a tiny case, where appeared, in thick and loose lines, but so crumbled that it was impossible to decipher them, a signature penned in frog green ink, like the kind Hungarian country folk use. I argued with Muchay:

"Can one really take a person's name and hide it in a case, like a simple ring or bill...?"

"Nothing more or less," the tavern owner replied.

"And what is the explanation of all this? So then, what is that name?"

"Neither you nor anyone can know it, since this name is now in my sole possession. You, sir, can find out what it is, but you cannot know it..."

"Mr. Muchay, are you mocking me?"

"Not in the least. That man lost his name and he himself, although he would like to, cannot know it now. It is absolutely impossible for him, as long as he does not have in his possession the signature that you see before you."

"But if he signed it, it will be easy for him to sign it again and again."

"No. The name is but one alone. Signatures, there are many of these, no doubt, but the name is only one out of all the signatures."

His unexpected billiard subtleties began to make my mind swim. Muchay, on the other hand, spoke without faltering. He lit his pipe with two flicks on his Croatian flint. He closed the steel case and led me down.

"The life of a man," he said, walking down the stairs, "is completely revealed in only one of his acts. The name of a man is revealed in only one of his signatures. To know that representative act is to know his true life. To know that representative signature is to know his true name."

"And on what grounds do you believe that the signature you possess is the representative signature of that man? What's more, what does knowing a person's true name matter? Doesn't one know everyone's true name?

"Listen, sir," argued Muchay, placing a prudent inflection on his words, "the true name of many people remains unknown. This is why the worker from Loeben, and not the owner of the factory where he worked, was imprisoned

"But do you know the crime he is accused of?"

"An assault on Regent Horthy."

Bajé los ojos, dando viento a mis órganos medianos y me quedé Vallejo ante Muchay.

I lowered my eyes, blowing air into my medium-sized organs and remained Vallejo facing Muchay.

RUIDO DE PASOS DE UN GRAN CRIMINAL

Cuando apagaron la luz, me dio ganas de reír. Las cosas reanudaron en la oscuridad sus labores, en el punto donde se habían detenido: en un rostro, los ojos bajaron a las conchas nasales y allí hicieron inventario de ciertos valores ópticos extraviados, llevándolos en seguida; a la escama de un pez llamó imperiosamente una escama naval; tres gotas de lluvia paralelas detuviéronse a la altura de un umbral, a esperar a otra que no se sabe por qué se había retardado; el guardia de la esquina se sonó ruidosamente, insistiendo en singular sobre la ventanilla izquierda de la nariz; la grada más alta y la más baja de un escalinata en caracol volvieron a hacerse señas alusivas al último transeúnte que subió por ellas. Las cosas, a la sombra, reanudaron sus labores, animadas de libre alegría y se conducían como personas en un banquete de alta etiqueta, en que de súbito se apagasen las luces y se quedase todo en tinieblas.

Cuando apagaron la luz, realizóse una mejor distribución de hitos y de marcos en el mundo. Cada ritmo fue a su música; cada fiel de balanza se movió lo menos que puede moverse un destino, esto es, hasta casi adquirir presencia absoluta. En general, se produjo un precioso juego de liberación y de justeza entre las cosas. Yo las veía y me puse contento, puesto que en mí también corcoveaba la gracia de la sombra numeral.

No sé quién hizo de nuevo luz. El mundo volvió a agazaparse en sus raídas pieles: la amarilla del domingo, la ceniza del lunes, la húmeda del martes, la juiciosa del miércoles, la de zapa del jueves, la triste del viernes, la haraposa del sábado. El mundo volvió a aparecer así, quieto, dormido o haciéndose el dormido. Una espeluznante araña, de tres patas quebradas, salía de la manga del sábado.

SOUND OF A MASTERMIND'S FOOTSTEPS

When they turned off the light, I got the urge to laugh. Things resumed their duties in the darkness, right where they had stopped: on a face, the eyes lowered to the nostrils and there they took inventory of certain missing optical values, promptly carrying them off; a ship scale imperiously called to a fish scale; three parallel raindrops stopped at the height of a door frame to wait for another that, no one knows why, had lagged behind; the guard on the corner blew his nose loudly, singularly insisting on the left window of his nose; and the highest and lowest step of a spiral staircase once again made signs alluding to the final passer-by who went up them. The things, in the shadow, resumed their duties, breathed to life by unleashed joy and behaving like people at a high-end gala where all of a sudden the lights went out and everything was left in the darkness.

When they turned off the light, a greater distribution of milestones and marks in the world was made manifest. Each rhythm went with its music; each trustworthy scale moved as little as a destiny can move, that is, until acquiring an almost absolute presence. In general, a gorgeous play of freedom and justice among things in the world emerged inside me. I saw them and grew content, since the grace of the numeral shadow was bucking in me, too.

I don't know who let there be light again. The world once more crouched down in its worn out skin: yellow Sunday, ash Monday, humid Tuesday; judicious Wednesday, scheming Thursday, somber Friday, raggedy Sunday. The world reappeared as usual, at rest, sleeping, or pretending to be asleep. A hair-raising spider, with three broken legs, came out of Saturday's sleeve.

CONFLICTO ENTRE LOS OJOS Y LA MIRADA

Muchas veces he visto cosas que otros también han visto. Esto me inspira una cólera sutil y de puntillas, a cuya íntima presencia manan sangre mis flancos solidarios.

—Ha abierto sol, —le digo a un hombre.

Y él me ha respondido:

—Sí. Un sol flavo y dulce.

Yo he sentido que el sol está, de veras, flavo y dulce. Tengo deseo entones de preguntar a otro hombre por lo que sabe de este sol. Aquel ha confirmado mi impresión y esta confirmación me hace daño, un vago daño que me acosa por las costillas. ¿No es, pues, cierto que al abrir el sol, estaba yo de frente? Y, siendo así, aquel hombre ha salido, como desde un espejo lateral, a mansalva, a murmurar, a mi lado: «Sí. Un sol flaco[4] y dulce». Un adjetivo se recorta en cada una de mis sienes. No. Yo preguntaré a otro hombre por este sol. El primero se ha equivocado o hace broma, pretendiendo suplantarme.

—Ha abierto sol, —le digo a otro hombre.

—Sí, muy nublado, —me responde.

Más lejos todavía, he dicho a otro:

—Ha abierto sol.

Y éste me arguye:

—Un sol a medias.[5]

—¿Dónde podré ir que no haya un espejo lateral, cuya superficie viene a darme de frente, por mucho que yo avance de lado y mire yo de frente?

A los lados del hombre van y vienen bellos absurdos, premiosa caballería suelta, que reclama cabestro, número y jinete. Mas los hombres aman poner el freno por amor al jinete y no por amor al animal. Yo he de poner el freno, tan sólo por amor al animal. Y nadie sentirá lo que yo siento. Y nadie ha de poder ya suplantarme.

CONFLICT BETWEEN THE EYES AND THE GAZE

Quite often I have seen things that others have seen as well. This fills me with subtle and tiptoeing vexation, in whose intimate presence my supportive sides flow with blood.

"The sun has broken through," I say to a man.

And he replies:

"Yes. A sweet and tawny sun."

I have felt that the sun is, truly, tawny and sweet. So I get the urge to ask another man what he knows about this sun. He has confirmed my impression and this confirmation causes me pain, a dull pain that aggravates my ribs. Is it not, then, true that as the sun broke through, I was facing it? And, like this, that man has come, as if from a rear-view mirror, close up to murmur at my side: "Yes. A sweet and scrawny sun." An adjective is cut out from each of my temples. No. I shall ask another man about this sun. The first has made a mistake or is joking, trying to undermine me.

"The sun has broken through," I say to another man.

"Yes, quite cloudy," he responds.

Still further away, I said to another:

"The sun has broken through."

And this one argues with me:

"A half-baked sun."

"Where might I go to avoid a rear-view mirror, whose surface comes to smack me in the face, no matter how far I push on sidelong and gaze straight ahead?"

Alongside Man, beautiful absurdities come and go, a plodding cavalry on the move, in need of a leading ox, number and rider. Yet men love to hit the brakes out of love for the rider and not out of love for the animal. I must hit the brakes, out of love only for the animal. And no one will feel what I feel. And now no one will be able to undermine me.

MAGISTRAL DEMOSTRACIÓN DE SALUD PÚBLICA

Recuerdo muy bien cuanto pasó en el Hotel Negresco de Niza. Pero, por raro que parezca, hacer el relato de lo acontecido allí, me es absolutamente imposible. Hartas veces he querido —a fuerza y revólver en mano—relatar este recuerdo o esbozarlo siquiera, sin poder conseguirlo. Ninguna de las formas literarias me han servido. Ninguno de los accidentes del verbo. Ninguna de las partes de la oración. Ninguno de los signos puntuativos. Sin duda existen cosas que no se ha dicho ni se dirá nunca o existen cosas totalmente mudas, inexpresivas e inexpresables. ¿Existen cosas cuya expresión reside en todas las demás cosas en el universo entero, y ellas están indicadas a tal punto por las otras, que se han quedado mudas por sí mismas? Ya ni siquiera les queda nombre para indicarse y son ante las urnas, como si no existieran localmente.

He trazado, arrogando mi sentimiento, algunos dibujos, a la fuerza y revólver en mano. He golpeado una piedra protegiéndome de mástiles. He pulsado una cuerda, poniéndome en la hipótesis de poder traducir lo del Negresco, si no por medio de palabras, al menos, por medios plásticos o musicales en mitos de inducción.[6] Mi impotencia no ha sido entonces menos angustiosa. Un instante, en el son de mis pasos me pareció percibir algo que evocaba la ya lejana noche del Hotel Negresco. Cuando he pretendido someter ese fluido de mis pasos a un preconcebido plan de expresión, el ruido perdía toda sugestión alusiva al fugitivo tema de memoria.

Salí del español. El francés, idioma que conozco mejor, después del español, tampoco se prestó a mi propósito. Sin embargo, cuando oía hablar a un grupo de personas a la vez, me sucedía una cosa semejante a lo de mis pasos: creía sentir en este idioma, hablado por varias bocas simultáneamente, una cierta posibilidad expresiva de mi caso. Diré, así mismo, que las palabras *devenir*, *nuance*, *cauchemar* y *coucher* me atraían, aunque solamente cuando formaban frases y no cada una por separado. ¿Cómo manifestarme por medio de estas cuatro palabras inmensas y en movimiento, extrayendo de ellas su contagio elocutivo, sin sacarlas de las frases en que estaban girando como brazos? Además, las otras voces con las que iban enlazadas, algo debían tener de simpatía semántica hacia mis ideas y emociones del Negresco, puesto que su compañía comunicaba valor a los cuatro vocablos que he señalado.

Un día, una muchacha inglesa, bonita e inteligente, me fue presentada en la calle. El amigo que me la presentó, a quien le dije luego que la niña era bonita, me dijo:

MASTERFUL DEMONSTRATION OF PUBLIC HEALTH

I remember quite well all that happened in the Negresco Hotel of Nice. But, strange as it may seem, it's absolutely impossible for me to tell the story of what happened there. Too many times I have wanted—by force and with revolver in hand—to recount this memory or even sketch it out, to no avail. Not one literary form has been of any use to me. None of the verb's inflections. None of the parts of the sentence. None of the punctuation marks. Without a doubt, there exist things that have not been said and will not be said or there exist things that are totally mute, inexpressive and inexpressible. Do there exist things whose expression resides in all other things in the universe that are so indicated by the others, which have stayed mute by themselves? They don't even have a name anymore and, when facing the ballot-boxes, it's as if they didn't exist in their own district.

Possessing my feeling, I have sketched out a drawing, by force and with revolver in hand. I have beaten a stone protecting myself from masts. I have plucked a chord, situating myself in the hypothesis of being able to translate the Negresco ordeal, if not with words, then at least, by evocative or musical means in myths of inducement. My impotence has not been any less distressing. One time, I thought I perceived something in the sound of my footsteps, which recalled that now distant night in the Negresco Hotel. When I tried to submit that flow of my footsteps to a preconceived plan of expression, the noise was losing all allusive suggestion to the fleeting topic of the memory.

I left Spanish. French, the language I know best, after Spanish, did not lend itself to my purpose either. However, when I heard a group of people speaking all at once, something similar to hearing my footsteps happened to me: I thought I felt that this language, spoken by various mouths simultaneously, expressed my case. I will say, likewise, that the words *devenir, nuance, cauchemar* and *coucher* attracted me, though only when they formed phrases and not each one on its own. How can I express myself with these four immense words in motion, extracting from them their elocutionary contagiousness, without removing them from the phrases in which they were rotating like the booms of cranes. What's more, the other words with which they were interwoven must have had some kind of semantic sympathy with my ideas and emotions relating to the Negresco, since their company imparted value to the four words I have already pointed out.

One day, a young English girl, pretty and smart, was introducing me to people on the street. The friend who introduced her to me, the one who I later told the girl was pretty, said to me:

—Vous volulez coucher avec elle?

—Comment?

—Volulez-vous coucher avec Whinefree?

Entonces fue que la palabra francesa *coucher* y la inglesa Whinefree me parecieron de súbito emitir juntas, por boca de mi amigo, una suerte de vagos materiales léxicos, capaces tal vez de facilitarme el relato de mi recuerdo de Niza. Esto explica por qué, algún tiempo después, me refugié en el inglés. Tomé, al alzar, *Meanwhile* de Wells. Al llegar, reunido y en orden, al último párrafo de *Meanwhile*, me asaltó un violento y repentino deseo de escribir lo sucedido en el Negresco. ¿Con qué palabras? ¿Españolas, inglesas, francesas?... Las palabras inglesas *red*, *staircase*, *kiss*, se destacaban del último párrafo del libro de Wells y me daban la impresión de significar, no ya las ideas del autor, sino ciertos lugares, colores, hechos incoherentes relativos a mi recuerdo de Niza. Un calofrío pasó por el filo de mis uñas.

¿No será que las palabras que debían servirme para expresarme en este caso, estaban dispersas en todos los idiomas de la tierra y no en uno solo de ellos?

Diversas circunstancias, el tiempo y los viajes me fueron afirmando en esta creencia. En el idioma turco no hallé ninguna palabra para el caso, no obstante haberlo buscado mucho. ¡Qué estoy diciendo! Las voces que iban ofreciéndoseme en cada una de las lenguas, no venían a mi reclamo y según mi voluntad. Ellas venían a llamarme espontáneamente, por sí mismas, asediándome en forma obsesionante, de la misma manera que lo habían hecho ya las voces francesas e inglesas, que he citado.

Aquí tenéis el vocabulario que logré formar con vocablos de diversos idiomas. El orden inmigrante en que están colocados los idiomas y las palabras de cada idioma, es el cronológico de su advenimiento a mi espíritu. Cuando se me reveló la última palabra del rumano *noap* que se presentó simultáneamente con el artículo, tuve la impresión de haber dicho, al fin, lo que quería decir hacia mucho tiempo: lo ocurrido en el Hotel Negresco.

El vocabulario es éste:

Del lituano: fûta - eimufaifesti - meilla - fautta - fuin - joisja - jaet tä - jen - ubo - fannelle.

Del ruso: mekiy - chetb - kotoplim - yakl - eto - caloboletba - aabhoetnmb - ohnsa - abymb - pasbhtih - ciola - ktec tokaogp - oho - accohianih - pyeckih - teopethle - ckol - ryohtearmh.

"Vous volulez coucher avec elle?"

"Comment?"

"Vous volulez coucher avec Whinefree?"

So it was that the French word *coucher* and the English word *Whinefree* suddenly seemed to jointly emit, through my friend's mouth, a sort of vague lexical material, recalling my memory of Nice. This explains why, some time afterwards, I took refuge in English. I took, at random, *Meanwhile* from Wells. As I reached, bound together and in order, the final paragraph of *Meanwhile*, I was assaulted by a violent and sudden desire to write what happened at the Negresco. With what words? Spanish, English, French?... The English words *red, staircase, kiss* stood out in the final paragraph of the book by Wells, and they gave me the impression of signifying, not the ideas of the author, but certain places, colors, and events all incoherent with regard to my memory of Nice. A chill ran over the edge of my fingernails.

Might it not be that the words supposed to help me express myself in this case were spread throughout all the languages of the land and not in only one of them?

Different circumstances, time, and travel continued to confirm this belief. In the Turkish language I never found a word for the case, despite having sought it for quite some time. What am I saying! The words that came to me in each language didn't come on command or even at my request. They called me spontaneously, on their own, obsessively seizing me, in the same way that the French and English words that I've already mentioned had done.

Here you have the vocabulary that I managed to form with words from different languages. The immigrant order, in which the languages and words from each language are placed, is chronological according to their advent in my spirit. When the last word from the Romanian *noap* was revealed to me, presented simultaneously with an article, I had the feeling that I had said, at last, what I wanted to say for a long time: what happened in the Negresco Hotel.

This is the vocabulary:

From Lithuanian: fûta - eimufaifesti - meilla - fautta - fuin - jois ja - jaettä - jen - ubo - fannelle.

From Russian: mekiy - chetb - kotoplim – yaki - eto - calobo letba - aabhoetnmb - ohnsa - abymb - pasb htih - ciola - ktectokaogp - oho - accohianih - pyeckih - teopethle - ckol - ryohtearmh.

Del alemán: den - fru - borte - sig - abringer - shildres - fusande - mansaelges - foraar - violinistinden - moerke - fierh - dadenspiele.

Del polaco: âr - sandbergdagar - det - blivit - veder - börande - tva - stora - sig - ochandra.

Del inglés: red - staircase - kiss - and - familiar - life - officer - mother - broadcasting - shoulder - formerly - two - any - photographer - at - rise.

Del francés: devenir - nuance - cauchemar - coucher.

Del italiano: Coltello - angolo - io - piros - copo.

Del rumano: unchiu - noaptea.

Esta caprichosa jerga políglota me da la impresión de expresar aproximadamente mi emoción de los Alpes marítimos. Solamente me resta dejar constancia de dos circunstancias, de dos masas de guerra, de dos cortes al sesgo. Primeramente, ninguna de las múltiples voces que la forman, puede, por separado, traducir mi recuerdo de Niza. En segunda confianza, el poder de expresión de este vocabulario reside, especialmente, en el hecho de estar formado en sus tres cuartas partes sobre raíces arias y el resto sobre raíces semitas.

From German:	den - fru - borte - sig - abringer - shildres - fusande - mansaelges - foraar - violinistinden - moerke - fierh - dadenspiele.
From Polish:	âr - sandbergdagar - det - blivit - veder - börande - tva - stora - sig - ochandra.
From English:	red - staircase - kiss - and - familiar - life - officer - mother - broadcasting - shoulder - formerly - two - any - photographer - at - rise.
From French:	devenir - nuance - cauchemar - coucher.
From Italian:	coltello - angolo - io - piros - copo.
From Romanian:	unchiu - noaptea.

This fickle polyglot lingo approximated my emotion from the maritime Alps. I only need to certify two circumstances, two warring masses, two courts on a pitch. First off, none of the multiple words that make it up can, on its own, translate my memory from Nice. In second face, the ability to express this vocabulary resides, especially, in the fact that three quarters of it has been formed on Aryan roots and the rest on Semitic roots.

LÁNGUIDAMENTE SU LICOR

Tendríamos ya una edad misericordiosa, cuando mi padre ordenó nuestro ingreso a la escuela. Cura de amor, una tarde lluviosa de febrero, mamá servía en la cocina el yantar de oración. En el corredor de abajo, estaban sentados a la mesa mi padre y mis hermanos mayores. Y mi madre iba sentada al pie del mismo fuego del hogar. Tocaron la puerta.

—¡Tocan a la puerta! —mi madre.

—¡Tocan a la puerta! —mi propia madre.

—¡Tocan a la puerta! —dijo toda mi madre, tocándose las entrañas a trastes infinitos, sobre toda la altura de quién viene.

—Anda, Nativa, la hija, a ver quien viene.

Y, sin esperar la venia maternal, fuera Miguel, el hijo, quien salió a ver quién venía así, oponiéndose a lo ancho de nosotros.

Un tiempo de rúa contuvo a mi familia. Mama salió, avanzando inversamente y como si hubiera dicho: las partes. Se hizo patio afuera. Nativa lloraba de una tal visita, de un tal patio y de la mano de mi madre. Entonces y cuando, dolor y paladar techaron nuestras frentes.

—Porque no le dejé que saliese a la puerta, —Nativa, la hija—, me ha echado Miguel al pavo. A su pavo.[7]

¡Qué diestra de subprefecto, la diestra del padre, revelando, el hombre, las falanjas[8] filiales del niño! Podía así otorgarle las venturas que el hombre deseara más tarde. Sin embargo,

—Y mañana, a la escuela, —disertó magistralmente el padre, ante el público semanal de sus hijos.

—Y tal, la ley, la causa de la ley. Y tal también la vida.

Mamá debió llorar, gimiendo apenas la madre. Ya nadie quiso comer. En los labios del padre cupo, para salir rompiéndose, una fina cuchara que conozco. En las fraternas bocas, la absorta amargura del hijo, quedó atravesada.

Mas, luego, de improviso, salió de un albañal de aguas llovedizas y de aquel mismo patio de la visita mala, una gallina, no ajena ni ponedora, sino brutal y negra. Cloqueaba en mi garganta. Fue una gallina vieja, maternalmente viuda de unos pollos que no llegaron a incubarse. Origen olvidado de ese instante, la gallina era viuda de sus hijos. Fueron hallados vacíos todos los huevos. La clueca después tuvo el verbo.

LANGUIDLY HIS LIQUEUR

We must have been at a helpless age, when my father ordered our entrance to school. A Priestess of Love, one rainy afternoon in February, mom was serving a prayer-time snack in the kitchen. In the downstairs hallway, my father and older brothers were sitting at the table. And my mom was about to sit down next to the household hearth itself. Someone knocked on the door.

"Someone's knocking on the door!" my mother.

"Someone's knocking on the door!" my own mother.

"Someone's knocking on the door!" my whole mother said, plucking her entrails on infinite frets, over the whole height of who's here.

"Go, Nativa, the daughter, to see who's there."

Without waiting for maternal consent, Miguel outside, the son, who left to see who had arrived like this, opposing us breadthwise.

A time of thoroughfare contained my family. Mom went out inversely moving forward and as if she had said: the parts. A patio was made outside. Nativa was crying over such a guest, over such a patio and over my mother's hand. Then and when, pain and palate roofed our foreheads.

"Because I didn't let him go out the door," Nativa, the daughter, "Miguel has kicked me out of the cocoon. Out of his cocoon."

What a righthand of the sub-prefect, the righthand of my father, revealing, the man, the filial falanxes of the boy! He could grant the fortune that the man would later desire. However:

"And tomorrow, to school," the father masterfully expounded, before the weekly audience of his kids.

"And thus, the law, the cause of the law. And thus also life."

Mom must have cried, the mother barely groaning. No one wanted to eat anymore. A thin spoon that I know fit in the lips of the father, only to come out broken. The son's absorbed bitterness got stuck in the fraternal mouths.

But later, unexpectedly, a hen, not a distant or an egg-laying hen, but a brutal and black one, came out of a rain gutter and from that same patio of the evil guest, it clucked in my throat. It was an old hen, maternally widowed by some chicks that didn't manage to incubate. Origin forgotten in that instant, the hen was a widow of her children. All the eggs were found empty. The broody one later had the last word.

Nadie la espantó. Y de espantarla, nadie dejó arrullarse por su gran calofrío maternal.

—¿Dónde están los hijos de la gallina vieja?

—¿Dónde están los pollos de la gallina vieja?

¡Pobrecitos! ¡Dónde estarían!

No one startled her. And startling her, no one stopped cooing for her great maternal chills.

"Where are the old hen's children?"

"Where are the old hen's chicks?"

Poor little things! Where could they be!

VOCACIÓN DE LA MUERTE

El hijo de María inclinóse a preguntar:

—¿Qué lees?

El doctor alzó los ojos y lanzó una mirada de extrañeza sobre su interlocutor. Otros escribas se volvieron al hijo de María y al sabio rabino.

La asistencia al templo, aquel día era escasa. Se juzgaba a un griego por deuda. El acreedor, un joven sirio del país del Hernón, aparecía sentado en el plinto de una columna del pórtico y, por todo alegato antes sus jueces, lloraba en silencio.

—Leo a Lenin, —respondió el doctor, abriendo ante el hijo de María un infolio, escrito en caracteres desconocidos.

El hijo de María leyó mentalmente en el libro y ambos cambiaron miradas, separándose luego y desapareciendo entre la multitud. Al volver a Nazareth, el hijo de María encontró a su cuñado, Armani, disputando por celos con su mujer, Zabadé, hermana menor del hijo de María. Ambos esposos, al verle, se irritaron más, porque le odiaban mucho.

—¿Qué quieres?

El hijo de María estaba muy abstraído y se estremeció. Volviendo en sí, tornó a la calle, sin pronunciar palabra. Tuvo hambre y se acordó de sus primos, los buenos hijos de Cleofás.

—Jacobo, ¡tengo hambre!

—Me llaman por teléfono. Volveré, —respondióle Jacobo, en el hebreo dulce y axilado de la antigua Galilea.

Vino la tarde y hacia tres días que el hijo de María no tomaba ningún alimento. Fue a ver pasar a los obreros que solían volver de Diocesarea en las tardes y se dispersaban en las encrucijadas de Nazareth, unos hacia el Oeste, por las faldas apacibles del Carmelo, cuyo último pico abrupto parece hundirse en el mar; otros hacia las montañas de Samaria, más allá de las cuales se extiende la triste Judea, seca y árida. Se acercó a un muro y se acodó en la rasante. Estaba fatigado y sentía el corazón más vacío que nunca de odios y amores y más incierto que nunca el pensamiento.

El hijo de María cumplía aquel día treinta años. Durante toda su vida había viajado, leído y meditado mucho. Su familia le odiaba, a causa de su extraña manera de ser, según la cual desechaba todo oficio y toda preocupación de la realidad. Rebelde a las prácticas gentilicias y aldeanas, llegó a abandonar su oficio de carpintero y no tenía ninguna vocación ni orientación concreta. En su casa le llamaban *idiota*, porque,

VOCATION OF DEATH

The son of Mary leaned in and asked:

"What are you reading?"

The doctor raised his eyes and shot a surprised look at the speaker. Other scribes returned to the son of Mary and the wise rabbi.

Attendance at the temple that day was spare. A Greek man was judged for his debt. The creditor, a young Syrian from the land of Hermon, was seated at the base of a column in the portico and, due to all the allegations before the judges, he wept in silence.

"I'm reading Lenin," the doctor replied, opening a pamphlet written in foreign characters in front of the son of Mary.

The son of Mary read to himself from the book and both exchanged gazes, later separating and disappearing into the crowd. Upon return to Nazareth, the son of Mary ran into his brother-in-law, Armani, who was arguing out of jealousy with his wife, Zabade, the younger sister of the son of Mary. Both spouses grew more irritated when they saw him, out of their deep hatred for him.

"What do you want?"

The son of Mary was lost in thought and he shuddered. Coming to, he took to the street without uttering a word. He was hungry and remembered his cousins, the good children of Cleophas.

"Jacob, I'm hungry!"

"There's a phone call for me. I'll be right back," Jacob replied to him in that sweet and winged Hebrew of ancient Galilee.

Evening came and it had been three days since the son of Mary had eaten anything. He went to watch the workers who would return from Diocaesarea and disperse through the intersections of Nazareth, some towards the West, through the gentle skirts of Mt. Carmel, whose final abrupt peak seems to submerge into the sea; other towards the mountains of Samaria, beyond which sad Judea rests, dry and arid. He went up to a wall and leaned against it. He was exhausted—his heart more than ever felt void of hatred and love, and his thought, more than ever uncertain.

The son of Mary turned thirty years old that day. Throughout his life, he had traveled, read and meditated a great deal. His family hated him, due to his strange demeanor, in which he rejected every profession and concern with reality. A rebel against the practices of townsfolk, he eventually abandoned his job as a carpenter and no longer had any vocation or concrete direction. In his house, they called him an *idiot*,

en realidad parecía acéfalo. Varias veces estuvo a punto de perecer de hambre y de intemperie. Su madre le quería por *pobre de espíritu* más que a los otros vástagos. Con frecuencia desaparecía sin que se supiese su paradero. Volvía con una hiena salvaje en los brazos, desgarrada la veste, mirando en el vacío y llorando en ocasiones. Acostumbraba también traer una rama de la higuera de los lugares santos de la edad patriarcal, con cuyas flores frotaban sus hábitos los finos y espirituales terapeutas de la vida devota.

El hijo de María alcanzó a ver una gran piedra, cerca de él, y fue a sentarse en ella. Anochecía.

Entonces, salió de Nazareth, por la rúa desierta y pedregosa, un grupo de personas de extraño aire vagabundo. Venía allí el barquero Cefas, de Cafarnaúm y su suegra Juana; Susana, mujer de Khousa, intendente de Antipas, e Hillel, el de los aforismos austeros, maestro que fue del hijo de María. En medio de todos, avanzaba un joven de gran hermosura y maneras suaves. Hillel decía preocupado:

—El reposo en Dios, he aquí la idea fundamental de Philon de Alejandría. Además, para él, como para Isaías y aún para el mismo Enoch, el curso de las cosas es el resultado de la voluntad libre de Dios.

Al advertir al hijo de María, sentado en una piedra, Susana se le acercó y le habló. Pero el hijo de María no respondió: justamente en ese instante, acababa de morir. Hillel siempre engolfado en sus cavilaciones, tuvo una repentina exaltación visionaria y, dirigiéndose al joven de gran hermosura, que iba con ellos, le dijo, en el dialecto siriaco, estas palabras inesperadas:

—¡Ya eres, Señor, el Hijo del Hombre! ¡En este momento, Señor, empiezas a ser el hijo del hombre! En este momento, Señor, empiezas a ser el Mesías, anunciado por Daniel y esperado por la humanidad durante siglos.

—Ya soy el hijo del Hombre, el enviado de mi Padre —respondió el joven de las maneras suaves y la gran hermosura, como si acabase de tener un revelación por espacio de treinta años esperada.

En torno de su cabeza judía, empezó a diseñarse un azulado resplandor.

because in all reality he seemed brainless. He almost died from hunger and from exposure several times. His mother loved him more than her other children because he was *poor in spirit*. He often disappeared without anyone knowing his whereabouts. He returned with a wild hyena in his arms, his clothes torn to shreds, staring into space and sometimes weeping. He also used to bring home the branch of a fig tree from one of the holy places of the patriarchal age, the flowers of which refined spiritual therapists of devout life had rubbed against their habits.

The son of Mary managed to see a great stone, not far from him, and he went to sit on it. Night was falling.

Then, from Nazareth a group of people with a strange vagrant air left on the deserted and stony path. The boatman, Cephas of Capernaum, came over there and his mother-in-law, Juana; Susana, the wife of Kousa, the governor of Antipas, and Hillel, the one that always had an austere aphorism, who was the mentor of the son of Mary. In front of everyone, a young man with striking beauty and mild manners stepped forth. Worried, Hillel said:

"Rest in God, behold the fundamental idea of Philon of Alexandria. What's more, for him, like for Isaiah and even for Enoch himself, the course of things is the result of God's free will.

As she noticed the son of Mary, seated on a stone, Susana went up and spoke to him. But the son of Mary did not reply: at that very moment he died. Hillel, always prone to pondering, experienced a sudden visionary exaltation and, turning to the young man of striking beauty who was with them, he said, in a Syrian dialect, these unexpected words:

"You, Lord, are now the Son of Man! In this moment, Lord, you begin to be the son of man! In this moment, Lord, you begin to be the Messiah, proclaimed by Daniel and awaited by humanity for centuries."

"I am the son of Man sent by my Father," replied the young man of striking beauty and mild manners, as if he had just had a revelation thirty years in the making.

Around his Jewish head, a bluish glow began to appear.

Libretas adicionales

Muchos pensamientos habrá que colocar directamente en el texto. Los demás, se los colocará en fin del libro, bajo el título «notas». Los pensamientos precedidos de 3 puntos de interrogación (???), habrá, quién sabe, que colocarlos en *El Arte y la Revolución.*—*César Vallejo*

❂

1926

+++ — Amigo Alfonso Reyes, Señor Ministro Plenipotenciario: tengo el gusto de afirmar a usted que, hoy y siempre, toda obra de tesis, en arte como en vida, me mortifica.

+++ — El artículo que toca a las masas, es un artículo inferior. Si solo toca a las élites, se acusa superior. Si toca a las masas y a las élites, se acusa genial, insuperable.

Si Beethoven se queda en las aristocracias espirituales y permanece inaccesible a las masas, peor para él.

+++ — América Latina.

Ahí tenéis dos palabras que en Europa han sido y son explotadas por todos los arribismos concebibles. América Latina. He aquí un nombre que se lleva y se trae de uno a otro bulevar de París, de uno a otro museo, de uno a otra revista tan meramente literaria como intermitente.

En nombre de América Latina consiguen hacerse ricos, conocidos y prestigiosos. América Latina sabe de discursos, versos, cuentos, exhibiciones cinemáticas, con música, pastas, refrescos y humores de domingo. En nombre de América Latina se merodea en torno a las oficinas europeas de explotación de humildades infatuables de América, en busca de difusión de un folklor y una arqueología que se trae por las crines a servir aprendidos apotegmas de sociología barata. En nombre de América Latina se juega el peligroso rol diplomático de oratoria, susceptible de ser engatusado, en banquetes y aniversarios, a favor de flamantes quimeras convencionales de la política europea.

Para todo esto se prestan estas dos palabras. De ellas sacan gran provecho personal todos aquellos que nada pueden hacer por cuenta

Additional Notebooks

Many thoughts will have to be placed directly in the text. The rest of them will be placed at the end of the book, under the title 'notes'. The thoughts preceeded by three question marks (???) will have to be placed— —who knows?—in *Art and Revolution*. —*César Vallejo*

1926

+++ — My friend Alfonso Reyes, Mr. Minister Plenipotentiary: it is my pleasure to affirm to you sir that, today and always, all working theses, in art as in life, mortify me.

+++ — The object that reaches the masses is an inferior object. If it only reaches the elite, it's considered superior. If it reaches the masses and the elite it's considered genius, unbeatable.

If Beethoven stays put in the spiritual aristocracies and remains inaccessible to the masses, too bad for him.

+++ — Latin America.

There you have two words that have been exploited in Europe by every conceivable social ambition. Latin America. Here we have a name that's carried away and brought back from one boulevard of Paris to the next, from one museum to the next, from one magazine to the next, merely as literary as they are intermittent.

In the name of Latin America they manage to get rich, become well-known and prestigious. Latin America knows lectures, verses, tales, film debuts with music, pasta, beverages and humor on Sunday. In the name of Latin America someone prowls though the European offices that extract the easily infatuated humility of America in an attempt to publish a folklore and archeology that get yanked by their manes for the use of memorized apothegms on cheap sociology. In the name of Latin America they play the dangerous diplomatic role of the orator who, at banquettes and anniversaries, is easily sweet-talked into favoring the flaming conventional chimeras of European politics.

For all this these two words suffice. All those who can't do anything

propia, sino agarrándose al país de su procedencia y a antecedentes y referencias de familia.

Hasta Maurice Barrès, precisamente el Barrès del «culto del yo», ha aprovechado de América Latina.

+++ — Todo lo que llevo dicho aquí es mentira.

+++ — No quiero referir, describir, girar, ni permanecer. Quiero coger a las aves por el segundo grado de sus temperaturas y a los hombres por la lengua dobleancho de sus nombres.

1929-1930

+++ — La piedad y la misericordia de los hombres por los hombres. Si a la hora de la muerte de un hombre, se reuniese la piedad de todos los hombres para no dejarle morir, ese hombre no moriría.

+++ — El puro y desadaptado que choca con el mundo de las farsas y de las apañucias.

+++ — El actor que un día cesó de ser él para ser uno de los personajes que encarnaba en escena.

??? — He visto tres obreros trabajar y hacer un perno: eso es socialismo de la producción.

He visto a cuatro compartir una mesa y un pan: eso es socialismo del consumo.

+++ — Los bandidos religiosos, al ser regenerados, devienen todos sin dios.

+++ — Una nueva poética: transportar al poema la estética de Picasso. Es decir: no atender sino a las bellezas, estrictamente poéticas, sin lógica,

by themselves benefit greatly from them, clinging on to their country of birth, background and family records.

Even Maurice Barrès, the same Barrès from the "cult of the self," has reaped benefits from Latin America.

+++ — Everything I've said here is a lie.

+++ — I don't want to refer, describe, turn, or persist. I want to clutch birds to the second degree of their temperatures and men by the doublewide tongue of their names.

1929-1930

+++ — The mercy and compassion of men for men. If at a man's moment of death, all the mercy of all the men were mustered up to keep him from dying, that man would not die.

+++ — The pure and unadapted one who bumps into the world of farce and slight of hand.

+++ — The actor who one day stopped being himself in order to be one of the characters that he used to act out on stage.

??? — I have seen three workers collaborate and make a screw: that is the socialism of production.

I have seen four share a table and some bread: that is the socialism of consumption.

+++ — Religious crooks, upon rebirth, are all born godless.

+++ — A new poetic: to transport Picasso's aesthetic to the poem. That is, not to address anything but strictly poetic beauty, without logic, or

ni coherencia, ni razón. Como cuando Picasso pinta a un hombre y, por razones de armonía de líneas o de colores, en vez de hacerle una nariz, hace en su lugar una caja o escalera o vaso o naranja.

+++ — Para las almas de absoluto, la muerta es una desgracia intemporal, una desgracia vista de aquí, de allá, del mundo, del cielo, del instante y del futuro y del pasado. Para los seres materialistas, ello no es más que una desgracia vista de este mundo: como ser pobre, caerse, ponerse en ridículo, etc.

+++ — Yo quiero que mi vida caiga por igual sobre todas y cada una de las cifras (44 kilos) de mi peso.

1930

+++ — Mi metro mide dos metros; mi kilo pesa una tonelada.

+++ — No es poeta el que hoy pasa insensible a la tragedia obrera. Paul Valèry, Maeterlinck, no son.

+++ — El hombre que nació viejo y murió niño: la edad para atrás.

+++ — La risa por cosquillas y la risa por alegría moral. Rabelais.

+++ — Los ojos acostumbrados al cinema y los ojos acostumbrados a la lejanía.

??? — Los intelectuales son rebeldes, pero no revolucionarios.

+++ — Su mirada tiene el tamaño que hay de un violín al punto en que muere su sonido a la distancia.

coherence, or reason. Like when Picasso paints a man and, for reasons of harmony in line and color, instead of making a nose for him, he makes in its place a box or a stairway or a glass or an orange.

+++ — For the souls of the absolute, death is an everlasting disgrace, a disgrace seen from here, from there, from the world, from the heavens, from the moment and from the future and from the past. For those materialistic beings, it is just a disgrace seen from this world: like being poor, falling, making a fool of oneself, etc.

+++ — I want my life to be sprinkled evenly over each and every number (44 kilos) of my weight.

1930

+++ — My meter is two meters long; my kilo weighs a ton.

+++ — He who today walks by the tragedy of the worker unaffected is not a poet. Paul Valèry, Maeterlinck, they are not.

+++ — The man who was born old and died young: aging backwards.

+++ — Laughter from tickling and laughter from moral joy: Rabelais.

+++ — The eyes accustomed to the cinema and the eyes accustomed to distance.

??? — Intellectuals are rebels, but not revolutionaries.

+++ — Her gaze is the size of a violin just when its sound dies in the distance.

+++ — La muerte de una persona no es, como se cree, una desgracia. La desgracia está en otra cosa.

+++ — El amor me libera en el sentido que *puedo* dejar de amar. La persona a quien amo debe dejarme la libertad de poder aborrecerla en cualquier momento.

+++ — La aviación en el aire, en el agua y en el espíritu. Sus leyes en los tres casos son diversos. El espíritu vuela cuando pesa y se hunde más en sí mismo. Más grávido es un espíritu, más alto y más lejos vuela.

??? — Todo empieza siempre por el principio.

??? — La mecánica es un medio o disciplina para realizar la vida, pero no es la vida misma. Esa debe llevarnos a la vida misma, que está en el juego de sentimientos o sea en la sensibilidad: Walt Whitman, Vallejo.

??? — La ciudad más grande del mundo: Moscú. La justicia, el amor universal.

+++ — Yo amo a las plantas por la raíz y no por la flor.

+++ — El perro que por fidelidad, no consintió que se acercase nadie a curar la herida de su amo. Este, naturalmente, murió.

+++ — La naturaleza crea la eternidad de la sustancia. El arte crea la eternidad de la forma.

+++ — Nadie muere sino después de haber hecho alguna cosa interesante. Ese o aquel ha hecho algo interesante, puesto que *ahora muere.*

+++ — The death of a person is not, as is believed, a disgrace. Disgrace is something else.

+++ — Love frees me in the sense that I *am able to* stop loving. The person I love should give me the freedom to be able to abhor her at any moment.

+++ — Aviation in the air, in the water and in the spirit. Its laws in each of the three cases are different. The spirit flies when it's heavy and it sinks deeper into itself. The heavier the spirit, the higher and further it flies.

??? — Everything always starts at the beginning.

??? — Mechanics is a medium or discipline to carry out life, but it is not life itself. It should take us to life, which is in the set of feelings or rather in the sensibility: Walt Whitman, Vallejo.

??? — The greatest city in the world: Moscow. The justice, the universal love.

+++ — I love plants by their root and not their flower.

+++ — The dog that out of loyalty never let anyone come close to treat the wound of his owner. The latter, naturally, died.

+++ — Nature creates the eternity of Substance. Art creates the eternity of Form.

+++ — No one dies except after having done something interesting. This guy or that one has done something interesting, since *he's dying now*.

+++ — Las artes (pintura, poesía, etc.) no son solo éstas. Artes son también comer, beber, caminar: todo acto es un arte. Resbalón hacia el dadaísmo.

+++ — Mi amargura cae jueves.

+++ — Es curioso: creí que ese hombre era yo. Es igualito a mí. A tal punto que cuando volví la cara, casi estaba seguro de que era yo y casi choco conmigo mismo.

+++ — La misma vía que lleva, trae.

??? — Artísticamente, *socialismo* no es lo mismo que *humanismo*.

1931-1932

??? — El caso más elocuente de solidaridad social, es ver varios obreros que levantan una gran piedra.

+++ — El único que dice la verdad es el mentiroso.

+++ — Cuando leo, parece que me miro en un espejo.

+++ — Ça va la pluie?
Le moi de Mai est le plus antipathique du monde.

+++ — Mis anteojos se han parado (como un reloj).

+++ — Espinoza parece disfrazado de él mismo, de Espinoza.

+++ — The arts (painting, poetry, etc.) are not just these. There are also the arts of eating, drinking, walking: every act is an art. The slippery slope towards Dadaism.

+++ — My bitterness falls on Thursday.

+++ — It's strange: I thought that that man was me. He's just like me. To the point that when I turned my head, I was almost sure that he was me and I almost ran into myself.

+++ — The same street that unfolds there leads here.

??? — Artistically, *socialism* is not the same as *humanism.*

1931-1932

??? — The most eloquent case of social solidarity is to see several workers lifting a giant stone.

+++ — The only one who tells the truth is the liar.

+++ — When I read, it seems like I see myself in a mirror.

+++ — Happy with the rain?
May is the most unpleasant month ever, anywhere.

+++ — My eye glasses have stopped (like a clock).

+++ — Espinoza seems disguised to himself, as Espinoza.

+++ — Je m'aperçois bien qu'en ce moment on mange dans mon cœur.

+++ — Tengo ganas de escribir una cartita a todos, diciéndoles ¡qué bueno!

+++ — El dice: Ponte serio para que hagan lo que pides.
Y yo le digo: Lo harán no porque me ponga serio, sino porque lo que pido es justo.

+++ — Siento como crecen mis uñas.

+++ — Il est si difficile de tirarse un pedo.

+++ — Siento como crecen mis barbas en sueño.

+++ — Hace un frío teórico y práctico.

+++ — Escribí un verso en que hablaba de un adjetivo en el cual crecía hierba. Unos años más tarde, en París, vi en una piedra del cementerio Montparnasse un adjetivo con hierba. Profecía de la poesía.

+++ — El retrato de toda persona, lo encuentra siempre en el reservado.

??? — La ventaja del cinema está en que nosotros vemos cara a cara a los artistas, mientras que ellos no nos ven.

1933-1934-1935

+++ — Todos son héroes en alguna cosa.

+++ — I am well aware that right now someone is eating out my heart.

+++ — I've got the urge to write a note to everyone, saying—that's great!

+++ — He says: Get serious so they do what you ask them to.
And I tell him: They will do it not because I get serious, but because what I ask of them is fair.

+++ — I feel my fingernails grow.

+++ — Il est si difficile to pass gas.

+++ — I feel my whiskers growing in a dream.

+++ — A theoretical and practical cold has set in.

+++ — I wrote a line where I spoke about an adjective that was sprouting grass. A number of years later, in Paris, I saw on a headstone in the Montparnasse cemetery an adjective covered with grass. Prophesy of poetry.

+++ — The portrait of every person is always found in the private room.

??? — The advantage of the cinema is that we see the artists face to face, while they don't see us.

1933-1934-1935

+++ — Everyone is a hero at something.

+++ — Mi anarquía simple, mi gran dolor compuesto de alegrías.

+++— Va a hacer caca y por eso se pone los anteojos.

+++— Va al reservado y por eso se pone los lentes.

+++— Escribir un poema un poema: «Señores: tengo el honor de decir a ustedes que estoy muy bien…» Y comunicar luego el estado de mis "affaires" y demás.

+++— Volver a escribir los poemas: «Murió Lucas, mi cuñado, etc.» «Y "Mi autorretrato».

+++ — Un camelot débite sa marchandise –l'éloquence populaire et l'esprit de la foire. Scène à traiter dans *Vestiare*.

+++ — El metropolite Pierre, successeur du patriarche Thakou, et chef actuel de l'église orthodoxe russe, está en harmonie con el soviet. Les prêtes russes émigrés se sont placés sous l'autorité du patriarche de Constantinople. Espéce de schisme au sein de l'Église russe.

+++ — Le petit Prince Paul amené à une parade militaire, en tant qu'héritier du trône, pousa des cris d'épouvante è la vue des soldats, des chevaux, des tanks, etc.

+++ — Una estética teatral nueva: una pieza en que el autor convive, él y su familia y relaciones, con los personajes que él ha creado, que toman parte en su vida diaria, sus intereses y pasiones. No se sabe o se confunden los personajes teatrales con las personas vivas en la realidad.

+++ — My simple anarchy, my great pain composed of joy.

+++— He is going to take a poop and that is why he wears his glasses.

+++— He is going to the private room and that is why he wears his eye-glasses.

+++— Write a poem: "Gentlemen: I have the honor of telling you that I am just fine..." and then communicate the state of my affairs and the rest.

+++— Rewrite the poems: "My brother-in-law, Lucas, has died, etc." and "My Self Portrait."

+++ — A peddler hawks his goods—popular eloquence and the spirit of the street fair. A scene to address in *Vestiare*.

+++ — Pierre the metropolitan, successor of the patriarch Thakou and current head of the Russian Orthodox Church, is in harmony with the Soviet. The emigrant Russian priests have put themselves under the authority of the Constantinople patriarch. A kind of schism in the heart of the Russian Church.

+++ — Little prince Paul, when taken to a military parade, given that he was the inheritor of the throne, let out blood-curdling shouts upon seeing the soldiers, the horses, the tanks, etc.

+++ — A new theatrical aesthetic: a piece in which the author cohab-its—he, his family and his relatives—with the characters he has created, who take part in his daily life, his interests and passions. It's hard to tell or easy to confuse the theatrical characters with living people in reality.

+++ — Oyendo a Beethoven, una mujer y un hombre lloran ante la grandeza de esa música. Y yo les digo: si son ustedes los que tienen en su corazón esta grandeza.

+++ — Una estética nueva: poemas cortos, multiformes, sobre momentos evocativos o anticipaciones, como *L'Opérateur* en cinema de Vertof.

+++ — Todos corren de su propio pensamiento. El que baja una escalera, marcha en un tren, pasa por la calle, etc., lo que hace es correr de su pensamiento.

+++ — El sitio o lugar o paisaje o camino del mundo, por donde nadie ha pasado nunca y donde nada ha sucedido nunca.

??? — El chico que dijo, señalando el sexo de su madre: mamá, tienes pelo aquí.

La madre le dio un manazo: ¡chut! mozo liso.

El chico vio, sin embargo, una cosa existente y su conocimiento fue roto y controvertido por su propia madre, cuya palabra le merecía toda fe.

Aquí está la raíz de la farsa social y de los fracasos de la historia y de las luchas entre los hombres.

1936-1937

+++ — Todos esconden un revólver contra mí.

+++ — El hombre que no lloró nunca en sus 80 años de vida.

+++ — La incomprensión de España sobre los escritores sudamericanos que, por miedo, no osaban ser indoamericanos, sino casi totalmente españoles (Rubén Darío y otros).

Lorca es andaluz. ¿Por qué no tengo yo el derecho de ser peruano? ¿Para qué me digan que no me comprenden en España? Y yo, un aus-

+++ — Upon hearing Beethoven, a woman and a man cry before the greatness of that music. And I say to them: but it's you who in your heart have this greatness.

+++ — A new aesthetic: short poems, of varied form, about evocative and anticipatory moments, like *L'Opérateur* in the cinema of Vertof.

+++ — Everyone runs from his own thought. He who comes down the stairs, steps onto a train, walks through the street, etc., what's he doing is running from his thoughts.

+++ — The spot or place or landscape or way of the world, through which no one has ventured and where nothing has happened.

??? — The boy who said, pointing to his mother's sex: mom, you've got hair down there.

The mother gave him a good smack: Shush! you sassy kid.

The boy, nonetheless, saw something real and his knowledge was broken and retorted by his own mother, whose word deserved complete faith.

This is the root of social farce and of the failures of history and of the struggles of men.

1936-1937

+++ — Everyone holds a hidden gun to me.

+++ — The man who never cried in the 80 years of his life.

+++ — Spain's incomprehension of South American writers who, out of fear, did not dare to be Indo-American, but almost completely Spanish (Rubén Darío, *et al.*).

Lorca is Andalucian. Why don't I have the right to be Peruvian? Why do they say they don't understand me in Spain? And I, an Austrian

tríaco o inglés, comprenderán los giros castizos de Lorca y Cº.

+++ — ¡Cuidado con la substancia humana de la poesía!

29 de marzo de 1938

+++ — Cualquier que sea la causa que yo tenga que defender ante Dios, más allá de la muerte, tengo un defensor: Dios.

or Englishman, am to understand the purebred turns of Lorca and Co.

+++ — Careful with the human substance of poetry!

March 29, 1938

+++ — Whatever the case may be that I must defend before God, beyond death, I have a counsel for the defense: God.

Apéndice

I

Arte de tendencia (bolchevique, fascista).

Arte de propaganda —d°—.

Arte libre (socialista, proletario, imperialista, burgués, monarquista, consciente o subconsciente).

II

Freudismo o subconsciencia en arte: superrealismo.

Razón o control consciente en arte: arte ruso de hoy o arte revolucionario.

III

Romanticismo: arte ruso de hoy.

Realismo: arte ruso de hoy, Zola.

Verdadismo: Vallejo, Neruda.

Verismo o sincerismo: Israti, Remarque.

Fotografismo

Simbolismo y *Alegorismo* escolar

Dadaísmo

Expresionismo o directismo e inmediatismo.

IV

Sentido histórico o dialéctico de la revolución: Heine, Kipling, Rilke, Jlebnikov en Rusia.

V

La palabra en la poesía.

La idea en la poesía.

La emoción en la poesía.

Emoción natural: un ocaso.

Emoción vital: una caída en la calle (Knut Hamsun).

Emoción artística:

VI

La fórmula en el arte.

El truco en el arte.

La manera

El estilo (Véase Orrego).

Appendix

I

Trend Art (Bolshevik, Fascist).

Propaganda Art –d^{ism}.

Free Art (socialist, proletariat, imperialist, bourgeois, monarchist, conscious or subconscious).

II

Freudism or subconscious in art: surrealism.

Reason or conscious control in art: Russian art of today or revolutionary art

III

Romanticism: Russian art of today.

Realism: Russian art of today, Zola.

Truthism: Vallejo, Neruda.

Honestism or sincerism: Israti, Remarque.

Photographism

Symbolism and scholastic Alegorism

Dadaism

Expressionism or directism and immediatism.

IV

Historical or dialectic meaning of the revolution: Heine, Kipling, Rilke, Klebnikov in Russia.

V

The word in poetry.

The idea in poetry.

The emotion in poetry.

Natural emotion: a twilight.

Vital emotion: a fall in the street (Knut Hamsun).

Artistic emotion:

VI

Formula in art.

Trickery in art.

Manner

Style (See Orrego)

La técnica
La dialéctica en la técnica: perpetua elaboración: Mariátegui sobre
    Vallejo.

VII

La ciencia del arte: saber escribir: Poe, Valéry, Goethe, Walt Whitman.
Empirismo del arte.
Peligros de la ciencia y limitación empírica.

VIII

El tema: arte ruso.
Arte atemático: surrealismo.

IX

Destino del futurismo: en poesía, en pintura, en cinema.
Destino del cubismo

X

Fatalismo, determinismo y libre arbitrio.
Ultimas consecuencias socialistas del marxismo.
Dificultades del todismo profesional del obrero en el socialismo.

XI

El arte según Marx: reflejo de la economía.
El arte según la sociología clásica.
El arte según Kant y Hegel.
El arte según Freud.

XII

Carácter profesional del artista.
El iniciado y el no iniciado.
Hay un secreto profesional brahmánico en arte, ¿inaccesible al no
    iniciado?
¿No lo hay? No —dice el dadaísmo.
Virtualidad artística de todo hombre: el pueblo ruso.
Libertar el arte hasta matarlo —dice Vallejo hablando de Erik Satie.

XIII

El arte como producción económica.
El artista como obrero y sujeto de producción y consumo.

Technique
Dialectic in technique: perpetual development: Mariátegui on Vallejo.

VII

The science of art: knowing how to write: Poe, Valéry, Goethe, Walt
    Whitman.
Empiricism of art.
Dangers of science and empirical limitation.

VIII

Theme: Russian art.
A-thematic art: Surrealism.

IX

The fate of futurism: in poetry, in painting, in film.
The fate of cubism

X

Fatalism, determinism and free will.
Latest socialist consequences of Marxism.
Difficulties of professional unitarianism for the worker in socialism.

XI

Art according to Marx: reflection of the economy.
Art according to classical psychology.
Art according to Kant and Hegel.
Art according to Freud.

XII

Professional character of the artist.
The initiated and the uninitiated.
Is there a professional Brahmanic secret in art, inaccessible to the
    uninitiated?
Isn't there? "No" says Dadaism.
Artistic virtuality of every man: the Russian people.
"To free art until killing it" says Vallejo speaking of Erik Satie.

XIII

Art as economic production.
The artist as worker and subject of production and consumption.

El problema según el capitalismo.
Estado actual del problema.

XIV

Destino histórico de la obra de arte, a través de las estructuras sociales
      que se suceden en el tiempo: Zola, Hugo, Romain Rolland, etc.
Oportunismo de los artistas, según el vaivén social y político.
Boga u olvido intermitente, convencional e tendenciosa, de una obra,
      según las mareas políticas a los que ella sirve o ataca.

XV

La división del trabajo en el arte.
Poetas puros, que no son políticos y no se meten en otra cosa.
Poetas según Marx, que deben ser políticos militantes y conocerlo
      y vivirlo todo.
El socialismo repugna a la ley de la división del trabajo: (cosa
      imperialista: Taylor, Ford).

XVI

Todas las teorías son útiles para el artista, que debe ser y trabajar
      libremente.
Sin embargo, el artista debe saber a donde va y debe saber de que hay
      Chaplin, Eisenstein, etc.

XVII

El arte y el espíritu dialéctico.
Movimiento lógico: Morand.
Movimiento dialéctico: Vallejo.
Análisis marxista de Trilce y de otras obras vanguardistas francesas, rusas,
      yanquis e hispanoamericanas.

XVIII

Muerte de la paradoja.
Muerte del desplanto artístico.
Muerte del colmo.
Muerte de la prestidigitación.
Muerte de la clownería (circo y payasadas son invenciones o
      masturbaciones burguesas), Cocteau, Gómez de la Sema, etc.

The problem according to capitalism.
The actual state of the problem.

XIV

Historical fate in the work of art, through the social structures that
transpire over time: Zola, Hugo, Romain Rolland, etc.
Opportunism of artists, according to the social and political sway.
Intermittent, conventional and trendy popularity or unpopularity of a work
of art, according to the political tides which it defends or attacks.

XV

The division of labor in art.
Pure poets, who are not politicians and get involved in nothing else.
Poets according to Marx, should be militant politicians who know it all
and live it all.
Socialism rejects the law of the division of labor: (an imperialist thing:
Taylor, Ford).

XVI

All theories are useful to the artist, who should be and work freely.
However, the artist should know where he is going and should know
that there exists a Chaplin, Eisenstein, etc.

XVII

Art and the dialectic spirit.
Logical movement: Morand.
Dialectic movement: Vallejo.
Marxist analysis of Trilce and of other French, Russian, Yankee and
Hispanic American vanguard works.

XVIII

Death of the paradox.
Death of artistic abandonment.
Death of the last straw.
Death of prestige.
Death of clownery (circus and idiocies are bourgeois inventions or
masturbations), Cocteau, Gómez de la Sema, etc.

XIX

La grandilocuencia en arte.
Lo declamatorio: arenga, proclama.
Lo oratorio.
Lo apostolizante y sacerdotal en el arte.

XX

Neo simbolismo d'après-guerre.
Los valores y entidades económicas se tornan símbolos y hasta
Nueva: obrero, fuerza, máquina, taller, sindicato, huelga, soviet, bandera
    roja, la hoz, el martillo, la gavilla de trigo.

XXI

Análisis freudiano de *Fabla salvaje*, de «Myrto», de «Cera», de «Más allá
    de la vida y de la muerte» y de los «Muros» de *Escalas*.

XXII

La crítica.
No puede definirse lo que es el espíritu nuevo. Eso sería idiota: Basadre.
Hasta ahora mismo y en Rusia se emplea el método hegeliano de crítica.

XXIII

El arte y la cultura.
¿La técnica es signo de cultura, como quiere Marx? Estados Unidos,
    Francia, Alemania, Rusia, etc.
El poeta que dice avión, está obligado de ponerse a la altura del temple
    científico del espíritu o cultura creadora del avión.
De otro modo, no pasa de un *chauffeur* que conoce pero no comprende el
    avión que él pilota en su poema.
Primero nace la técnica y después, como reflejo, ¿nace el arte?
O primero nace el arte y luego, como consecuencia, la técnica de
    producción económica?
Lenin ha suscitado el arte proletario o al contrario.
Maiakovski: mis mejores maestros de poesía: Marx y Lenin

XXIV

Vanguardismo y seudo (bohemios anacrónicos 1830, no trabajan y
    trasnochan con drogas).

XIX

Grandiloquence in art.

The declamatory: lauds, proclaims.

The oratory.

The apostolizing and priestly in art.

XX

Neo symbolism d'après-guerre.

Values and economic organizations become symbols and even...

New: worker, strength, machine, workshop, syndicate, strike, Soviet,
   red flag, the sickle, the hammer, the wheat thresher.

XXI

Freudian analysis of *Savage Tale*, of "Mirtho", of "Wax", of "Beyond
   Life and Death" and of "Walls" in *Scales*.

XXII

Criticism.

One cannot define what the new spirit is. That would be idiotic: Basadre.

Up until now and in Russia the Hegelian method of criticism is used.

XXIII

Art and culture.

Is technique a sign of culture, as Marx says? United States, France,
   Germany, Russia, etc.

The poet who says airplane is obliged to rise up to the height of the
   scientific nature of the spirit or creative culture of the airplane.

Otherwise, he is merely a *chauffeur* who knows but doesn't
   comprehend the airplane he pilots in his poem.

Is technique born first and then, as a reflection, is art born?

Or is art born first and later on, as a consequence, the technique of
   economic production?

Lenin has given rise to proletariat art or the contrary.

Mayakovski: my best poetry teachers: Marx and Lenin.

XXIV

Avant-garde and pseudo (anachronistic bohemians of 1930,
   who don't work and stay up all night on dope).

XXV

La belleza de una selva y aquella de una urbe (Hugo y Proust).

XXVI

El teatro.

Cuarto muro teatral de D[ubois] en la Ópera Cómica para el *Pobre [marinero]* de Cocteau y Milhaud.

Cinema y teatro (Teatro Piscator)

Mimodrama, Orfeo, de Roger Ducasse, por Ida Rubinstein, en que los actores se expresan por gestos y solo son los coros y corifeos que cantan.

Melodrama, Hipodamia, Chemlovaco, drama musical hablado, tentado ya por Wagner y diverso de la Ópera.

Teatro del gesto de Cocteau.

Teatro del silencio de Maeterlinck.

XXVII

Expresionismo, expresar fielmente lo inmediato y actual, las ideas. Evitar la palabrería, la cosquilla verbal, busca lo espiritual.

Imaginismo o fantasismo, preciosidad mórbida, juego de palabra, sequedad de expresión, aliteraciones, sueños deformadores, rebusca deimágenes. Doscientas imágenes consagradas a la luna, por Essenin.

Unanimismo, Walt Whitman, Jules Romains.

No existe término general para designar a todas las escuelas de hoy.

Maurice Raynald dice: la sucesión al término «simbolismo», sigue vacante.

Constructivismo, volumen sobre todo.

XXV

The beauty of a jungle and that of a city (Hugo and Proust).

XXVI

Theater.

Four wall theater by D[ubois] in the Comic Opera for Cocteau and
    Milhaud's *Poor [sailor]*

Cinema ad theater (Piscato Theater)

Mimodrama, Orpheus, by Roger Ducasse, adapted by Ida Rubinstein,
    in which the actors express themselves with gestures and only the
    choruses and backup singers sing.

Melodrama, Hipodamia, Chemlovaco, a spoken musical play, already
    attempted by Wagner and others in the Opera.

Cocteau's theater of gesture.

Maeterlinck's theater of silence.

XXVII

Expressionism, to loyally express the immediate and actual, the ideas.
    To avoid wordiness, a verbal tickle, it searches for the spiritual.

Imagism or fantasism, morbid gorgeousness, word play, dryness of
    expression, alliterations, deformed dreams, eclectic images. Two
    hundred consecrated images of the moon, by Essenin.

Unanimism, Walt Whitman, Jules Romains.

There is no general term to designate all of today's schools. Maurice
    Raynald says: the progression of the term "symbolism" is still
    vacant.

Constructivism, volume above all else.

Translator's Notes

1. The word "antivital" is a neologism, based on the stem "vital" (vital, characteristic of life of living beings) and the prefix "anti-" (opposed to).

2. The word "periplan" appears to be a verbal neologism ("periplar"), based on the masculine noun "periplo" that refers to a trip, often returning to the point of departure, e.g. a round-trip. Likewise, it may also refer to a spiritual journey, and in ancient geography, it signified circumnavigation. The poet assigns a noun the function of an intransitive verb. Semantically, this simply means "the statues that are spread throughout the plaza, from one end to the other, walking all around it like people." The noun "circuit" has been chosen to replicate this function.

3. The phrase "un juego de dulce de hierro"—literally "a game of iron candy"—is apparently a colloquial expression for a children's game. Due to the unconfirmed nature of the expression, the name of a children's game recognizable to English language readers has been preferred.

4. González Vigil's edition reads "flavo y dulce", repeating "flavo" (tawny); whereas Priego's version reads "flaco" (skinny, slim, thin). Thus, either choice here sends the translation in a different direction. Eshleman interprets it as "flavo" and translates it as "fallow." The difficulty here resides in the fact that Vallejo is renown for making slight (graphical and/or phonetic) alterations. Whether this is a deliberate alteration made by the poet himself or a typographical error in Priego's version is another question. In the present volume—aware of the risk of reproducing an error—I have opted to follow Priego and reprint "flaco", since I believe that if this risk could preserve the complexity and subtlety of the original, then it is worth taking. In this way, "flaco" becomes "scrawny".

5. The expression "un sol a medias" plays off "media luna" (half moon); but an action that occurs "a medias" occurs *incompletely*. Moreover "a medias" exceeds the realm of the incomplete. It also refers to what is shoddy, not done well. Eshleman translates "a medias" as "incomplete" accounting for the denotative element at the expense of the connotative. I have highlighted the connotative meaning with "half-baked".

6. It is not clear what Vallejo means by "mitos de inducción". These

myths could be of "induction" (inferring a general conclusion from particular instances) or, as we prefer, of "inducement" (a matter that is presented by way of background to explain the principle allegations of a legal case).

7. The Spanish here is riddled with symbolic meaning. Vallejo evokes the "pavo" (turkey) and "pavo real" (peacock) in his sister Nativa's voice: "Miguel me ha echado al pavo. A su pavo." It is important to remember that Miguel, the poet's brother, died in 1915, affecting the young Vallejo who would eulogize him in several poems of *The Black Heralds* and *Trilce*. In Spanish the "pavo" appears in the phrase "la edad del pavo" that refers to the age of awkwardness in a young person's life as he or she enters the teenage years. In this light, it might be interpreted as "Miguel has thrown me into adolescence" (i.e. by dying at an early age and leaving me to fend for myself). Another line emerges from the interpretation of this expression as a play on "echarle gindes al pavo" (to throw [morello] cherries at the turkey), semantically "to embarrass". In this sense, it could mean "what was supposed to embarrass Miguel, embarrassed me instead." Translating the image of the turkey or the peacock here is virtually impossible, since the symbolism is—if not lost—then grossly deformed. The phrase used here—"kicked me out of the cocoon"—attempts to account for the idea of loss and the consequential hardship that the poet and his sister endured, while keeping the image in the realm of the animal kingdom.

8. The word "falanjas" is a neologism based on "falanjes." The word "falanxes"—replacing the "ph" with an "f"—reproduces the phonetic alteration which Vallejo intuits in the Spanish.

ROOF BOOKS

the best in language since 1976

Titles

- Andrews, Bruce. **Co**. Collaborations with Barbara Cole, Jesse Freeman, Jessica Grim, Yedda Morrison, Kim Rosefield. 104p. $12.95.
- Andrews, Bruce. **Ex Why Zee**. 112p. $10.95.
- Andrews, Bruce. **Getting Ready To Have Been Frightened**. 116p. $7.50.
- Arakawa, Gins, Madeline. **Making Dying Illegal**. 224p. $22.95.
- Benson, Steve. **Blue Book**. Copub. with The Figures. 250p. $12.50
- Bernstein, Charles. **Controlling Interests**. 80p. $11.95.
- Bernstein, Charles. **Islets/Irritations**. 112p. $9.95.
- Bernstein, Charles (editor). **The Politics of Poetic Form**. 246p. $12.95; cloth $21.95.
- Brossard, Nicole. **Picture Theory**. 188p. $11.95.
- Cadiot, Olivier. **Former, Future, Fugitive**. Translated by Cole Swensen. 166p. $13.95.
- Champion, Miles. **Three Bell Zero**. 72p. $10.95.
- Child, Abigail. **Scatter Matrix**. 79p. $9.95.
- Davies, Alan. **Active 24 Hours**. 100p. $5.
- Davies, Alan. **Signage**. 184p. $11.
- Davies, Alan. **Rave**. 64p. $7.95.
- Day, Jean. **A Young Recruit**. 58p. $6.
- Di Palma, Ray. **Motion of the Cypher**. 112p. $10.95.
- Di Palma, Ray. **Raik**. 100p. $9.95.
- Doris, Stacy. **Kildare**. 104p. $9.95.
- Doris, Stacy. **Cheerleader's Guide to the World: Council Book** 88p. $12.95.
- Dreyer, Lynne. **The White Museum**. 80p. $6.
- Dworkin, Craig. **Strand**. 112p. $12.95.
- Dworkin, Craig, editor. **The Consequence of Innovation: 21st Century Poetics**. 304p. $29.95.
- Edwards, Ken. **Good Science**. 80p. $9.95.
- Eigner, Larry. **Areas Lights Heights**. 182p. $12, $22 (cloth).
- Eisenhower, Cathy. would with and. 120p. $13.95
- Fitterman, Robert. **Rob the Plagiarist**. 108p. $13.95
- Fodaski, Elizabeth. Document. 80p. $13.95
- Gardner, Drew. **Petroleum Hat**. 96p. $12.95.
- Gizzi, Michael. **Continental Harmonies**. 96p. $8.95.
- Gladman, Renee. **A Picture-Feeling**. 72p. $10.95.
- Goldman, Judith. **Vocoder**. 96p. $11.95.
- Gordon, Nada. **Folly**. 128p. $13.95
- Gordon, Nada. Scented Rushes. 104p. $13.95
- Gottlieb, Michael. **Ninety-Six Tears**. 88p. $5.
- Gottlieb, Michael. **Gorgeous Plunge**. 96p. $11.95.
- Gottlieb, Michael. **Lost & Found**. 80p. $11.95.

- Greenwald, Ted. **Jumping the Line**. 120p. $12.95.
- Grenier, Robert. **A Day at the Beach**. 80p. $6.
- Grosman, Ernesto. **The XULReader: An Anthology of Argentine Poetry (1981–1996)**. 167p. $14.95.
- Guest, Barbara. **Dürer in the Window, Reflexions on Art**.
Book design by Richard Tuttle. Four color throughout. 80p. $24.95.
- Hills, Henry. **Making Money**. 72p. $7.50. VHS videotape $24.95. Book & tape $29.95.
- Huang Yunte. **SHI: A Radical Reading of Chinese Poetry**. 76p. $9.95
- Hunt, Erica. **Local History**. 80 p. $9.95.
- Kuszai, Joel (editor) **poetics@**, 192 p. $13.95.
- Inman, P. **Criss Cross**. 64 p. $7.95.
- Inman, P. **Red Shift**. 64p. $6.
- Lazer, Hank. **Doublespace**. 192 p. $12.
- Levy, Andrew. **Paper Head Last Lyrics**. 112 p. $11.95.
- Mac Low, Jackson. **Representative Works: 1938–1985**. 360p. $18.95 (cloth).
- Mac Low, Jackson. **Twenties**. 112p. $8.95.
- McMorris, Mark. **The Café at Light**. 112p. $12.95.
- Mohammad, K. Silem. The Front. 104p. $13.95
- Moriarty, Laura. **Rondeaux**. 107p. $8.
- Nasdor, Marc. **Sonnetailia**. 80p. $12.95
- Neilson, Melanie. **Civil Noir**. 96p. $8.95.
- Osman, Jena. **An Essay in Asterisks**. 112p. $12.95.
- Pearson, Ted. **Planetary Gear**. 72p. $8.95.
- Perelman, Bob. **Virtual Reality**. 80p. $9.95.
- Perelman, Bob. **The Future of Memory**. 120p. $14.95.
- Perelman, Bob. **Iflife**. 140p. $13.95.
- Piombino, Nick, **The Boundary of Blur**. 128p. $13.95.
- Price, Larry. **The Quadragene**. 72p. $12.95.
- Prize Budget for Boys, **The Spectacular Vernacular Revue**. 96p. $14.95.
- Raworth, Tom. **Clean & Will-Lit**. 106p. $10.95.
- Reilly, Evelyn. **Styrofoam**. 72p. $12.95.
- Retallack, Joan. Procedural Elegies/Western Civ Cont/. 120p. $14.95.
- Robinson, Kit. **Balance Sheet**. 112p. $11.95.
- Robinson, Kit. **Democracy Boulevard**. 104p. $9.95.
- Robinson, Kit. **Ice Cubes**. 96p. $6.
- Rosenfield, Kim. **Good Morning—MIDNIGHT—**. 112p. $10.95.
- Scalapino, Leslie. **Objects in the Terrifying Tense Longing from Taking Place**. 88p. $9.95.
- Seaton, Peter. **The Son Master**. 64p. $5.
- Shaw, Lytle, editor. **Nineteen Lines: A Drawing Center Writing Anthology**. 336p. $24.95
- Sherry, James. **Popular Fiction**. 84p. $6.
- Silliman, Ron. **The New Sentence**. 200p. $10.
- Silliman, Ron. **N/O**. 112p. $10.95.
- Smith, Rod. **Music or Honesty**. 96p. $12.95
- Smith, Rod. **Protective Immediacy**. 96p. $9.95
- Stefans, Brian Kim. **Free Space Comix**. 96p. $9.95

- Stefans, Brian Kim. **Kluge**. 128p. $13.95
- Sullivan, Gary. **PPL in a Depot**. 104p. $13.95
- Tarkos, Christophe. **Ma Langue est Poétique—Selected Works**. 96p. $12.95.
- Templeton, Fiona. **YOU—The City**. 150p. $11.95.
- Torre, Mónica de la. **Public Domain** 104 p. $13.95.
- Torres, Edwin. **The All-Union Day of the Shock Worker**. 112 p. $10.95.
- Torres, Edwin. **Yes Thing No Thing**. 128 p. $14.95.
- Tysh, Chris. **Cleavage**. 96p. $11.95.
- Ward, Diane. **Human Ceiling**. 80p. $8.95.
- Ward, Diane. **Relation**. 64p. $7.50.
- Watson, Craig. **Free Will**. 80p. $9.95.
- Watten, Barrett. **Progress**. 122p. $7.50.
- Weiner, Hannah. **We Speak Silent**. 76 p. $9.95
- Weiner, Hannah. **Page**. 136 p. $12.95
- Wellman, Mac. **Miniature**. 112 p. $12.95
- Wellman, Mac. **Strange Elegies**. 96 p. $12.95
- Wolsak, Lissa. **Pen Chants**. 80p. $9.95.
- Yasusada, Araki. **Doubled Flowering: From the Notebooks of Araki Yasusada**. 272p. $14.95.

ROOF BOOKS are published by
Segue Foundation
300 Bowery • New York, NY 10012
Visit our website at **seguefoundation.com**

ROOF BOOKS are distributed by
SMALL PRESS DISTRIBUTION
1341 Seventh Street • Berkeley, CA. 94710-1403.
Phone orders: 800-869-7553
spdbooks.org